Editorial

AS THE EDITOR of AirForces Monthly, I encounter a great many aircraft types but none can match the character or generate such enthusiasm as the F-4 Phantom. It has seen combat in numerous war zones, including Cyprus and Vietnam, and today the Israeli Phantom (or Kurnass) is still involved in air-to-ground operations against Lebanon. An Israeli F-4 pilot, who had also flown F-16s, told me recently that the Phantom… "squeaks, makes strange sounds, and you have to know how to fly it at low speed – but you will always remember it with passion".

Today, the F-4 Phantom is in operation with nine air forces and two of these countries — Greece and Turkey — are putting their aircraft through major upgrade programmes that could see them flying until 2020. While the Phantom could become the first combat aircraft to have a career life spanning over 60 years, it is already a legend. I hope you enjoy reading this Phantom Special as much as I enjoyed editing it.

ALAN WARNES, EDITOR, AIRFORCES MONTHLY

Phantom
The Legend

If ever there was an aircraft for all seasons, then the McDonnell Douglas F-4 Phantom II must rank as the leading contender. No other aircraft has achieved, or is ever likely to achieve, such a level of operational use within the West's air forces. Glen Sands and René J Francillon look at variants and operators.

AT THE HEIGHT of its service, the F-4 equipped 12 air forces around the world – from the decks of US carriers patrolling the oceans, to the deserts of the Middle East. No other aircraft in recent times has engaged in combat so frequently and in such a diverse range of climates.

The Phantom remains in service to this day, although reduced in numbers and in operators. But through upgrades, the 'Rhino', the 'Double Ugly', or simply the F-4 Phantom is still an aircraft to be reckoned with – and is set to continue in front-line service for a number of years, it will almost certainly see its 60th birthday as a front-line aircraft, just one more record for this amazing aircraft.

Birth of a Legend

The development of the F-4 can be traced back to October 1954, when McDonnell Douglas received an order for two prototypes designated YF4H-1 and -2. The first aircraft flew on May 27, 1958, from McDonnell Douglas' facility at Lambert-St Louis Municipal Airport. It was intended as a twin-engined, two-seat, long-range all-weather attack fighter for service with the US Navy but such were its capabilities that a combined total of 5,195 examples were built in the United States and under licence in Japan by Mitsubishi, and it served in a wide range of roles.

Preceded by the YAH-1 (not built) and two YF4H-1 prototypes, production versions of the Phantom II were given series letters A through

M (with the letters G, H, I, and L being skipped during production). Subsequent modifications resulted in variants being given series letter G (twice) N, S, and X, while their F type symbol was prefixed in numerous instances by status or special-purpose prefixes.

US Navy and USMC

The first US Navy fighter squadron selected to receive the Phantom was VF-101 based at Miramar, California, its first **F4H-1**, 148256, arriving on December 29, 1960. Designated Pacific Fleet Fighter Replacement Training Squadron, VF-101 received about 24 similar aircraft during the following eight weeks and set about training, with an initial complement of 46 pilots and Radar Intercept Officers (RIOs), some of whom later left to join other squadrons scheduled to fly the Phantom. A number of personnel were assigned to NAS Oceana in June 1961 to provide the core of a counterpart Atlantic Fleet Replacement Squadron, although new aircraft were not delivered there until August. Forming the Navy's Combat Readiness Air Wing (Replacement Air Group), VF-101 was joined by the second squadron, VF-121, the former moving to Key West NAS (with tail codes AD) and the latter taking its place at Miramar NAS (with tail codes NJ). The first operational Phantom squadron to be activated with F4H-1s was Navy Fighter Squadron VF-74 of the Atlantic Fleet. VF-114 of the Pacific Fleet followed soon after, as did VF-102, also of the Atlantic Fleet. As further squadrons were activated and re-equipped, VF-74 initially engaged in carrier qualification trials aboard USS *Saratoga*, and in August 1962 it became the first Phantom squadron to be operationally deployed to sea, joining USS *Forrestal* alongside F-8 Crusaders for a commission in the Mediterranean. Within a few days, VF-102 embarked in USS *Enterprise* and joined the Fleet in the Mediterranean. In September that year VF-114 was embarked in USS *Kitty Hawk* for a cruise in the Western Pacific. At that time it was normal practice in the US Navy for each Carrier Air Wing at sea to comprise two interceptor squadrons, the majority of such squadrons remaining based ashore in the United States and 'rotated' in turn for commission at sea. That same year, F4H-1s were delivered to the US Marine Corps in the attack role, Marine Corps Fighter Attack Squadron VMFA-314 receiving its first aircraft. This Squadron was almost immediately re-classified an all-weather unit (VMF[AW]-314), and was followed by the Marine Air Attack Training Squadron VMFAT-122.

In 1962, a change in American aircraft nomenclature came into effect, the early F4H-1Fs, a batch of 47 research and development Phantoms, became designated **F-4As**, and F4H-1s became **F-4Bs**. By the end of 1962, F-4Bs were deployed with three squadrons of the Navy, namely VF-74, VF-102 and VF-114, as well as VMF(AW)-314 and VMFAT-122 of

Above: *The sleek lines of the Phantom are portayed in this photo of a 56 Sqn Phantom FGR.2 off the coast of Cyprus, during its last Armament Practice Camp (APC) at Akrotiri.* AFM – DUNCAN CUBITT
Below: *The first Phantom, YF4H-1 BuNo 142259 made its maiden flight on May 27, 1958. It crashed on October 21, 1959, claiming the life of test pilot, Gerald (Zeke) Huelsbeck.* ALL PHOTOS, MCDD VIA RENE FRANCILLON UNLESS STATED

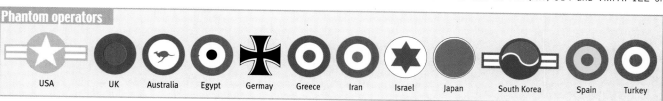

Phantom operators

| USA | UK | Australia | Egypt | Germay | Greece | Iran | Israel | Japan | South Korea | Spain | Turkey |

F-4A

Development aircraft powered by 10,350/16,150lb st (46.0/71.8kN) J79-GE-2s or -2As, the F-4A armament consisted of four Sparrow III SARH missiles in recesses beneath the fuselage, the air-to-air mission being the primary task. An additional Sparrow could be carried beneath each wing. Up to 16,000lb (7,257kg) of bombs, rockets, and other ordnance could be carried on four underwing and one centreline stations. For the strike role, a special weapon (nuclear) could be carried on the centreline. External tanks on the centreline and inboard wing stations boosted the fuel load from the 1,957 US gallons (7,408 litres) in six fuselage and two wing tanks to a maximum of 3,297 gallons (12,480 litres), whilst a retractable in-flight refuelling probe was provided in the forward starboard fuselage side.

F-4B

Powered by 10,900/17,000lb st (48.5/75.6kN) J79-GE-8s and fitted with revised air intake ramps, the F-4Bs were otherwise similar to late production F4H-1Fs. Provision was added for carrying four Sidewinder infra-red air-to-air missiles on wing racks and the internal fuel load was increased to 1,983 gallons (7,506 litres).

A total of 649 F-4Bs was delivered to the USN and USMC between June 1961 and March 1967; 29 of these were delivered to the USAF. In naval service, F-4Bs were fitted with chaff dispensers and more effective Radar Homing and Warning Systems (RHAWS) and Deception Systems (e.g. AN/ALQ-51 and AN/ALQ-100). Aircraft modified as drone directors, electronic aggressors with pod-mounted countermeasures and jammers, or permanently modified as test-beds respectively received DF-4B, EF-4B and NF-4B designations.

F-4J

After three modified F-4Bs were tested as YF-4Js, this version was adopted as the second and last fighter version for the USN and USMC. Powered by two 17,900lb (79.6kN) J-79-GE-10 engines, the F-4J had drooping ailerons and slotted stabilators to shorten take-off distance and reduce approach speed. Its AN/AJB-7 bombing system provided improved ground attack capability. Its AN/AWG-10 fire-control system was housed in an enlarged radome and incorporated an AN/APG-59 pulse-Doppler radar. Other changes included larger main wheels with 'thick' wings as used on Air Force aircraft, improved RHAW/countermeasure sets and an additional fuel cell in the rear fuselage to bring internal capacity to 1,998 gallons (7,525 litres). The VTAS (Visual Target Acquisition System) helmet sight and radar ground cooling fans were fitted to Blocks 45 and 46 F-4Js, with VTAS being retrofitted to most earlier aircraft. The first YF-4J flew on June 4, 1965. In all, 522 F-4Js were delivered to the USN and USMC between December 1966 and January 1972. Those modified as electronic aggressors became EF-4Js.

The second variant, an F4H-1 Block 7, BuNo 148390 (later redesignated F-4A) received a number of modifications that included the air intakes' straight lips, fixed ramps replaced by dual ramps, and an infra-red seeker beneath the nose.

the US Marine Corps.

By the time of the Tonkin Gulf incident in August 1964, 13 of the 31 Navy-deployable fighter squadrons were equipped with F-4Bs, whilst one had a mix of F-4Bs and F-4Gs, the latter aircraft being an interim production variant equipped with an approach power compensation system for use in automatic carrier landing mode, and one was converting from F-3Bs to F-4Bs. In addition, two RAG squadrons flew a mix of F-4As and F-4Bs. During the conflict in South-East Asia (see 'Phantoms in Vietnam, page 66-73), 22 Navy squadrons and a Marine squadron made 84 war cruises to the Gulf of Tonkin, including 51 with F-4Bs, one with F-4Gs and 32 with the more sophisticated **F-4Js**. The US Navy claimed 41 confirmed air combat kills, but 71 of its F-4s were lost in combat and 54 in operational accidents during wartime deployments.

Originally conceived in 1962, the first **RF-4B**, for the tactical reconnaissance role, made its maiden flight on March 12, 1965. The nose was lengthened to accommodate a much improved array of sensors and other electronics; however, the RF-4B carried no offensive armament, and flying controls were omitted from the rear cockpit. For night reconnaissance missions, photo-flash ejectors were fitted in either side of the rear fuselage. Unlike USAF RF-4Cs, the RF-4Bs retained the in-flight refuelling probe on the standard border side of the front fuselage. These were the longest-serving of all Phantoms, some remaining in service with the Marines until the

early 1980s. The first deliveries were made to Marine composite-reconnaissance squadron VMCJ-3 at El Toro MCAS, California, in May 1965, followed by VMCJ-1 at Iwakuni, Japan and VMCJ-2 at Cherry Point.

Towards the end of the 1970s, surviving RF-4Bs underwent a Service Life Extension Programme (SLEP). Known as Project SURE (Sensor Update Refurbishment Effort), this incorporated improved navigation and infra-red equipment. The first of the re-worked RF-4Bs was completed at North Island in 1977, and the last in 1981, each conversion being carried out at a unit cost of around $4.5 million. In the mid-1970s, when the Navy and Marine Corps' reconnaissance and ECM facilities were re-organised, all the RF-4Bs were re-assigned to a single Marine Corps fighter-reconnaissance squadron, VMFP-3, at El Toro, which provided temporary detachments overseas when required. As previously mentioned, the Marines also operated Phantoms in the conventional ground-support role, receiving their first example, an F4H-1, in June 1962. The Corps went on to operate a succession of variants, including the F-4B, F-4J, **F-4N** and **F-4S**. At one time, Phantoms equipped 15 active-duty fighter attack squadrons, two training squadrons and four reserve squadrons.

Marine Phantoms undertook a wide range of missions in the Vietnam War, losing 72 fighters and three RF-4Bs, the majority to ground fire. Marine crews claimed the destruction of three MiGs, though at these times the crews were on exchange with the USAF.

After the Vietnam war, both the US Navy and

An F-4B-6-MC, BuNo 148371 seen during the testing of conformal weapon carriage adaptors at China Lake.

Specially marked F-4Js of VX-4 and a QF-4N of the Naval Missile Center, Point Mugu show off their unusual colour schemes during June 1976.

the Marine Corps acquired new aircraft – the F-14 Tomcat and F/A-18 Hornet. While the Phantom still remained with the two services in large numbers, the aircraft's role was beginning to diminish, many F-4s being passed down to reserve and training units. The Phantom was finally withdrawn from the US Navy in 1987, VF-202, a reserve squadron, being the last to fly Phantoms in the interception role using the F-4S variant.

Marine Phantoms lasted slightly longer in service; indeed, at one time the F-4s were the only fighter aircraft within the Corps. The final fighters, F-4s of VMFA-112, were retired on January 18, 1992, though reconnaissance RF-4Bs were to remain for a few years longer. They finally departed to Cherry Point for parts and reclamation and eventual storage, having retired from front-line service with VMFP-3 on August 10, 1990.

United States Air Force

Early USAF evaluations of the Navy aircraft conclusively proved the superiority of the F-4 over current fighters, and swallowing its pride, the USAF ordered its own Phantoms. The Air Force designation F-110 was soon forgotten, and successive variants were procured, introducing more and more modifications to meet specific requirements. A number of F-4Bs underwent an initial evaluation at Edwards AFB in 1962, and were eventually delivered to the 4453rd Combat Crew Training Wing (CCTW) before returning to the US Navy after deliveries of the USAF's own **F-4Cs** had started. The F-4C (or F-110A as it was designated for a short time prior to the DoD standardisation of Service nomenclature) featured a number of airframe changes, as well as a switch to the J79-GE-15 engine. This engine featured a self-contained cartridge/pneumatic starter mounted on the lower wheel case – replacing the Navy's turbine-impingement system which used an external air supply. The Navy's low-section wheels were not suitable for Tactical Air Command's (TAC) asphalt runways, so the tyres were broadened, allowing anti-skid systems to be fitted. The Navy's air refuelling probe was discarded in favour of a dorsal receptacle to match the USAF KC-135 flying boom refuelling system. At the outset, it was USAF policy to crew the F-4C with two rated pilots, the front pilot being the Aircraft Commander (AC) and the rear pilot simply the Pilot. Later, the USAF adopted certain Navy training procedures, and the rear crew member was no longer a rated pilot, becoming a Weapons System Operator (WSO). The first F-4Cs to enter operational service were delivered to the four squadrons of the 12th Tactical Fighter Wing at MacDill AFB in 1962.

During the 15 years that the F-4C served with the USAF, it flew with the 8th, 12th, 18th, 35th, 52nd, 81st, 366th and the 401st Tactical Fighter Wings, the 57th Fighter Weapons Wing and the 58th Tactical Training Wing (as well as the Tactical Fighter Training Wing). Furthermore, the Air National Guard Squadrons of Arkansas, Illinois, Indiana, Louisiana, Hawaii, Michigan, Mississippi, Missouri and Texas also operated the type.

The USMC received 46 RF-4Bs between 1965-70 and these saw service, like so many Phantoms, in the Vietnam War. This example of VMFP-3, is seen taxiing into position at Yuma MCAS.

Numerous other examples served with a variety of test and evaluation establishments.

However, the F-4C was viewed only as an interim variant, and the 585 produced for USAF service were soon to be replaced by a more specialised variant, the F-4D. First flown in December 1965, F-4Ds did not reach combat units until 1967. Improvements to the aircraft included an ASQ-91 weapon release computer installed in the No 1 fuel tank bay, together with an ASG-22 lead-computing sight system – whilst an APQ-109 radar was mounted in the nose, giving an improved air-to-ground ranging capability. In the course of development trails with early F-4Ds, a considerably increased range of external stores was cleared and this variant was compatible from the outset with the Maverick Air to Ground Missile (AGM) and Falcon Air to Air Missile (AAM), as well as the emerging generation of laser-guided smart bombs. In due course, **F-4Ds** replaced the F-4Cs serving in Vietnam. The first victory for the improved variant came on June 5 when Major Everett T Raspberry of the 555th TFS downed a MiG-17 with an AIM-9 Sidewinder.

Many other victories were to follow, and F-4Ds were to register an impressive combat record in the war, although pilots complained about the lack of a fixed-gun armament. This was finally resolved in the **F-4E**, the most significant of all USAF Phantom variants. First flown on June 30, 1967, the F-4E was an improved variant of the D-model and was equipped with a Westinghouse AN/PQ-120 solid-state radar fire control system. Mounted internally was a M61A1 20-mm Vulcan cannon with 640 rounds, providing an effective close-in weapon for air combat. Entering USAF service in 1968 and reaching the combat zone in November that year, the F-4E became the most numerous version of the Phantom and, in its prime was widely used by the USAF and ANG. The first 30 were delivered without radar and the first 67 had no RHAW, but most were retrofitted with AN/APQ-120 and AN/APR-36/37. Remaining in production for 12 years, the F-4E was built for more air forces and in larger number than any other F-4 variant (with

'Choose your weapon' ... A great many more variations could be added to this early shot of F-4 weapon options; one of the aircraft's most significant points has been its multi-role capabilities.

KEN DELVE COLLECTION

959 going to the USAF and 428 being built for export customers). Export models were delivered without the nuclear weapon capability and, in some cases, with other restrictions. A number of new sensors and systems were retrofitted or added during production to maintain the operational capability of the variant.

Produced on such a large scale, it was inevitable that the USAF would develop the F-4E further. Experience in Vietnam showed the expanding need for the Suppression of Enemy Air Defences (SEAD) role, numerous aircraft having been downed to North Vietnamese SAMs. So emerged the **F-4G Wild Weasel** which featured the AN/APR-47 electronic warfare suite and AGM-88 HARM for the role of neutralising SAM-related air defence radars. The F-4Gs served in pairs as a hunter/shooter team or, as a director aircraft to F-16s in the fighter-bomber role. In the F-4G, the back-seater is an Electronic Warfare Officer (EWO) who navigates, assists with communications, and sets up the attack on SAM radars. The first aircraft reached the 37th TFW at George AFB, California, in October 1978. Other examples served with units at Spangdahlem, Germany, and Clark AB, Philippines.

The SAM killers had their finest moment in 1991 during Operation DESERT STORM when F-4Gs of the 35th Tactical Fighter Wing (Provisional) from Sheikh Isa Air Base, Bahrain, led early attacks against the Iraqi air defence network, firing numerous HARMs.

The USAF also required a tactical reconnaissance platform, with all air-to-air and conventional air-to-ground weapon systems deleted, the **RF-4C** was conceived as a photo and multiple-sensor reconnaissance aircraft. The first production-standard RF-4C flew on May 18, 1964, and entered service with the 33rd TRTS at Shaw AFB in September. During Operation DESERT STORM, RF-4Cs served alongside F-4Gs of the 35th TFW and with the 7740th Composite Wing at Incirlik AB, Turkey. LOROP-equipped RF-4C Phantoms also flew several hundred day reconnaissance missions including *Scud* hunts, their cameras providing a slant range for useful photography up to 55 miles (88.51km) on missions flown at 30,000ft (9,144m).

Despite the capabilities of the Phantom and the large numbers in service, the introduction of more modern types such as the F-15 and F-16 in the late 1970s and early 1980s saw the gradual withdrawal of the type from front-line

Above; *Three early-block F-4Cs formate alongside a KC-135A during their pre-delivery days. The aircraft are 63-7446 (top and now preserved at Speyer, Germany), 63-7524 (foreground and written off on December 12, 1969) and 63-7426 (middle, now preserved at Sheppard AFB).*
Below: *Three F-4Ds of the 194th FIS/144th FW/California ANG formate with a T-33A from the same unit.*

An F-4E of the 50th TFW, wearing a code 'B' during the Tactical Air Meet at RAF Wildenrath in June 1978. ALAN WARNES

RF-4C

Deliveries of 503 all-weather, day-night, high-low reconnaissance RF-4Cs were made to the USAF between May 1964 and January 1974. They had three camera stations in the nose and, at least initially, the capability of processing film in flight and ejecting cassettes. A photoflash ejection system was provided for night photography. In addition, they had an AN/APQ-99 or -162 forward-looking radar and could be fitted with AN/APQ-102 side-looking mapping radar or AN/AAS-18 infra-red reconnaissance set.

Powered by J79-GE-15s, RF-4Cs carried neither gun nor missiles but, unlike the RF-4B, they retained the provision for carrying a nuclear store on the centreline station. During their long service life with the USAF, RF-4Cs had their ECM capabilities steadily improved (notably through the addition of RHAWS and other sensors) and its other systems upgraded the nose.

and second-line units. The first to go were the F-4Cs when the 123rd FIS of the Oregon Air National Guard traded in its Phantoms in the autumn of 1989. One year later, the distinction of operating the final F-4D models fell to the 'Jayhawks' of the 127th TFS in Kansas, who transitioned to the F-16A/ADF in the summer of 1990, disposing of their F-4Ds in the process. The later generation, such as the F-4E, F-4G and RF-4C, remained into the mid-1990s, the final F-4Es being retired in 1991. Such was the importance of the missions the F-4Gs and RF-4C fulfilled, that the aircraft soldiered on past their predicted retirement dates. The F-4Gs of the 190th FIS Nevada ANG carried on until April 1996, and the RF-4Cs until March 1992 when the 12th TRS Blackbirds were decommissioned.

United Kingdom

The Royal Navy (RN) became the first overseas customer for the Phantom as the result of not being able to agree with the Royal Air Force on a joint specification for the proposed bi-service Hawker Siddeley P.1154 V/STOL strike attack aircraft. Negotiations for a British Phantom with Rolls-Royce Spey turbofan engines were held in January 1964, and an official go-ahead for the development was given by the government in July 1964, the original RN plan being to obtain 143 Phantoms. However, cuts in the aircraft carrier fleet resulted in reductions

to 137, then 110, and then only 50, plus seven options. In the event, 14 of the 50 production F-4Ks went straight to the RAF.

Royal Navy aircraft were designated **Phantom FG.1** (US designation F-4K) to indicate fighter and ground attack duties. The aircraft differed considerably from the US Navy's F-4J from which they were derived. The first YF-4K, XT595, flew on June 27, 1966, followed by XT596 on August 31. These early aircraft served in the experimental role, flying with the Royal Aircraft Establishment at Bedford and Boscombe Down. Flown by US civilian crews, the first three production RN Phantoms arrived at Royal Naval Air Station (RNAS) Yeovilton via the Azores on April 29, 1968. Initial crew training was undertaken by 700P Squadron, following which 892 Squadron was formed for carrier-based operations aboard HMS *Ark Royal*, and 767 Squadron handled training. Ultimately the requirement for crews was so small that this training task was handed over the RAF.

Delivery of the last FG.1s was completed on November 21, 1969. Under the command of Lt Cdr Brian Davis AFC, the squadron was commissioned on March 31, 1969, and in the process its aircraft adopted a large red fin flash and an omega symbol as their motif on the assumption that they would be the last fixed-wing RN flyers. At the time, HMS *Ark Royal* was undergoing a refit, which was not

completed until February 1970, so carrier qualification were made aboard the USS *Saratoga*.

Four FG.1s were embarked aboard the US carrier for a week of deck operations in October 1969. The training was interrupted when the carrier was put on alert in the Eastern Mediterranean during the Lebanon Crisis – during which time RN FG.1s flew a number of air defence sorties with resident F-4Js of VF-103 'Sluggers'. This exchange was the start of a number of cross-deck operations for USN and RN Phantoms crews, other deployments occurred aboard the USS *Enterprise*, *John F Kennedy*, *Forrestal* and *Nimitz*.

The primary role of the Phantoms aboard the *Ark Royal* was that of air defence and their secondary, ground attack. The dual tasking would see countless launches and the aircraft heavily committed to NATO, for which in July 1973 under exercise SALLY FORTH a record number of launches were achieved from the decks of the *Ark*.

On a more public side, 892 NAS took part in the *Daily Mail* Transatlantic Air Race in May 1969, but in the event was unsuccessful against an RAF Harrier team. By 1978, the *Ark Royal* had reached the end of her useful life and with the retirement of the carrier so FAA FG.1 operations were brought to a close, culminating with the squadron disbandment on December 15, 1978.

F-4G

Previously used for modified F-4Bs for the USN, the F-4G designation was next used to identify 134 F-4Es rebuilt as the ultimate USAF Wild Weasel defence suppression role and fitted with leading edge manoeuvring slats. Modified by McDonnell Aircraft, the first entered flight trials in December 1975. Subsequent aircraft were modified at the Ogden Logistics Center, Hill AFB, Utah. Primary armament consisted of AGM-45, AGM-78, and finally AGM-88 anti-radiation missiles, TV-guided or IIR (imaging infra-red) AGM-75 air-to-ground missiles and CBUs. For self-protection, F-4Gs retained the capability of carrying AIM-9s. A Performance Update Program (PUP) was undertaken in the late 1980s to upgrade the APR-38 radar warning and attack system to APR-47 standard, thus enabling F-4Gs to cope with new threats. F-4G drones are designated QF-4Gs

A USAF F-4G with inert AGM-78 Standard Anti-Radiation Missile wearing the 'WW' Wild Weasel tail code of the 37th TFW at the time.

Four Sparrows and four Sidewinders adorn this Phantom of 56 Squadron. KEN DELVE COLLECTION

It was intended that the **RAF's Phantom F-4Ms (FGR.2s** in service) would perform strike and reconnaissance roles with NATO's Second Tactical Air Force until replaced by the Jaguar, due to arrive in service in the early 1970s, whereupon the FGR.2s would replace the RAF's Lightnings in the air defence role. It was announced in July 1965 that an agreement had been reached for two YF-4Ms and 150 production FGR.2s in 1965-67. The first unit to fly the Phantoms was 228 Operational Conversion Unit (OCU) at Coningsby, which although formed in February 1968, did not receive its first aircraft until the following August. By October 1969, the RAF's order had been completed. Once again, the fixed-cost nature of the British contract reduced the number of Phantoms for the RAF from 150 to 118, but to make up the deficiency, 14 Royal Navy aircraft were delivered direct to the RAF.

The first RAF Phantom squadron was 6 Squadron at Coningsby, formed on May 7, 1969, with crews trained by 228 OCU. They were joined by 43 Squadron at Leuchars, 54 Squadron at Coningsby, 14 Squadron and 17 Squadron at Bruggen in Germany, joined later by 2 Squadron, formed at Laarbruch in December 1970, the latter as a tactical reconnaissance unit, the aircraft being equipped with a centre-line recce pod. By 1976/77 Phantoms were available in sufficient quantity to replace the Lightning F.2As then serving with the Germany-based 19 and 92

Squadrons at Wildenrath, close to the Dutch border. The distinction of receiving the first F-4 fell to 19 Squadron, which along with 92, was tasked to police the air defence identification zone (ADIZ) running along the East/West German border. Both squadrons provided a five-minute QRA alert, known as Battle Flight. Serving as part of the 2nd ATAF, the two squadrons daily flew fast and at low-level over Germany as a deterrent to any potential low-level Warsaw Pact strike aircraft.

The Phantoms of 19 and 92 were constantly on alert throughout the Cold War and would have been the first NATO aircraft into action had the Warsaw Pact ever launched an attack. With the ending of the Cold War and the reunification of Germany, the need for German-based RAF interceptors was gone and the two squadrons were withdrawn in 1991. The first to disband was 92 Squadron on July 5, 1991; No 19 followed on January 9, 1992. However, both squadrons were to be reborn as reserve Hawk units, but the Phantom's time had long since past. The arrival of Jaguars in Germany freed Phantoms to take on the UK air defence role; the first squadron to re-equip being 111 at Coningsby. Two other UK-based fighter units, 23 and 29 Squadrons, also received Phantoms. Later air defence armament included the improved BAe Sky Flash in 1979 and AIM-9L AAMs in the early 1980s.

Phantoms began operating in the Southern Hemisphere in 1982 when they bolstered the defences of the Falkland Islands, recaptured from Argentina, the aircraft being operated by 1435 Flight. In order to compensate for the loss of aircraft diverted to the Falklands, the RAF purchased 15 ex-USN/USMC F-4Js for European use. Retaining their J79 engines and the bulk of the American avionics, these non-standard machines arrived in Britain between August 1984 and January 1985, adopting the designation **F-4J(UK)**. Phantom ranks were thinned during the late 1980s by the conversion of squadrons to the Tornado F.3. The FG.1s were first to be pensioned off, followed by the F-4J(UK) in January 1991, while 75 of the FGR.2s received new BAe-built outer wing panels from 1987 onwards to extend their fatigue lives.

By the start of 1992, only 56 and 74 Squadrons at Wattisham remained, and both of

Phantom FG.1s served the Royal Navy for just over ten years. Here XT872 of 892 Sqn is seen at RNAS Yeovilton in September 1977. DAVE ALLPORT

Australia operated 24 leased USAF F-4Es for just over two years in the early-1970s. This aircraft, 69-0305, is now a QF-4G target drone, operated by the 82nd Aerial Targets Squadron at Tyndall AFB, Florida. MAP

them disbanded in the autumn, shortly after 1435 Flight on the Falkland Islands converted to Tornados. One Phantom remained flying within the UK, a FG.1 XT597 which served as a high-speed calibration platform with the Aircraft & Armament Evaluation Establishment at Boscombe Down but this too has now been retired to the embryo museum there.

Australia

A reluctant and short-term operator, the Royal Australian Air Force (RAAF) leased 24 USAF **F-4Es** to maintain an effective front-line attack force when its acquisition of 24 F-111Cs was delayed. The first five aircraft arrived at Amberley on June 15, 1970. Three similarly-sized batches were accepted in September and October. The USAF trained 120 RAAF air and ground crews on the F-4 and stationed personnel at Amberley to supervise acceptance of the aircraft and train the remaining technicians. One example, serving with No 82 (Bomber) Wing, was lost in service in 1971 during a night bombing practice, and under the terms of the agreement, Australia paid $2.7 million compensation to the USAF. The RAAF eventually gave up its Phantoms after the Australian Government agreed that work relating to the F-111's fatigue problems could recommence. In the autumn of 1972, the US offered to sell the remaining 23 F-4s, but the deal fell through. 'Repatriation' from Brisbane to Hill AFB, Utah, began with six aircraft on October 25, 1972, followed by a further batch of five on November 8. On June 1, 1973, the first six F-111s arrived, and on June 21, the last ex-RAAF Phantom arrived in the US.

Egypt

Delivered as a result of improving relations with the West in the late 1970s, and as much as a result of deteriorating relationships with its neighbour Libya, 35 early-production ex-USAF

F-4Es arrived in Egypt in September 1979. Included in the package with the F-4s were 350 AIM-9 Sidewinders, 70 AIM-7 Sparrow AAMs and 500 AGM-65A Maverick TV-guided ASMs. The Phantoms were assigned to two Egyptian Air Force (EAF) units, 76 and 88 Squadrons of the 222nd Tactical Fighter Brigade at Cairo West. The Phantoms were plagued with serviceability problems early in their operational career and at one stage, the squadrons were barely able to raise nine serviceable aircraft in a week. In an effort to resolve the situation, a US-led maintenance team provided technical assistance to EAF ground crews throughout the early 1980s.

The Phantoms were given a last chance in mid-1983 when a US-led team succeeded in boosting serviceability to 80%. As a result, Egypt decided to keep the aircraft. Of the remaining 33 aircraft, two were lost in operational accidents. Egypt received a further seven ex-USAF examples and is currently modifying its fleet with an improved version of the AN/APG-65 radar.

This upgrade and overhaul of the F-4s is taking place at NADep Cherry Point, North Carolina, although the programme has not been without its problems. Early aircraft were ferried to the US by Tracor contract crews who at one stage refused to continue the delivery process due to the EAF F-4s being in such poor condition. This resulted in one example remaining at RAF Lakenheath for nearly five months awaiting repair. However, the programme is continuing with McDonnell Douglas contract pilots, five examples being delivered at a time for modification and upgrades.

CURRENT EGYPTIAN AF UNITS		
222th Tactical Fighter Brigade		
F-4E	76 Sqn	Cairo-West
F-4E	88 Sqn	Cairo-West

Germany

Two squadrons (Geschwaders) of the Luftwaffe were assigned to the air defence role, and it was to replace its F-104Gs that West Germany decided on the F-4 at the end of the 1960s. Designated the **F-4F**, the 'Germanicised' Phantom was, in effect, a simplified version of the F-4E. Most of the classified items of American electronics – unavailable for export – were omitted, whilst the wings, rear fuselage, tail unit and engines were manufactured in West Germany and shipped to St Louis for assembly. The first flight took place in May 1975 and production deliveries took place between June that year and April 1976.

The F-4F entered service with the Luftwaffe's JG 71 'Richthofen' and JG 74 'Molders' in the interception role (30 aircraft on each unit) and with JaboG 35 and 36 in the fighter-strike role at Pferdsfeld and Rheine-Hopsten respectively (with 36 aircraft on each unit). Assuming a numerically greater importance in the Luftwaffe than in any other air forces, the **RF-4E** replaced the RF-104G and served with Aufklarungsgeschwader 51 'Immelmann' at Bremgarten and AG 52 at Leck (both with 30 aircraft). Four other RF-4Es were assigned to special operations, possibly for low-level flights along Warsaw Pact borders: the remainder were held in reserve. A total of 88 aircraft were ordered in 1968.

Following the dramatic changes within Germany, the Phantom fleet has undergone significant changes over the last few years. The current fleet is distributed among four Jagdgeschwader: JG 71 at Wittmund, JG 72 at Hopsten, JG 73 at Laage (serving alongside a squadron of 23 MiG-29s), and JG 74 at Neuberg. The Luftwaffe also has 24 F-4Fs located at Holloman AFB, New Mexico, where the aircraft serve within a combined US/Luftwaffe operational training unit for future Phantom aircrew. Delays in the Eurofighter programme have seen 110 F-4Fs put through an Improved Combat Efficiency (ICE) upgrade. The improvements provide a look-down/shoot-

F-4F

Optimised to Luftwaffe requirements, 175 F-4Fs were delivered between June 1973 and April 1976. Major assemblies were produced in Germany by MBB and VFW-Fokker, while the J79-MTU-17A engines were built under licence from General Electric by Motoren-und-Turbinen-Union München GmbH. An air-refuelling receptacle and Sparrow missiles were retrofitted under the PEACE RHINE programme, whilst the more recent ICE (Improved Combat Efficiency) programme instituted further upgrades.

Egypt acquired F-4Es in September 1979 and continues to operate two squadrons. VIA LON NORDEEN

CURRENT GREEK AF UNITS			
110th Combat Wing	F-4E	337MPK	Larissa
	RF-4E	348MTA	Larissa
117th Combat Wing	F-4E	338MPK	Andravida
	F-4E	339MPK	Andravida
(MPK = air interception/multi-role, MTA = tactical reconnaissance)			

former US Air National Guard examples. These fighters serve alongside approximately 19 of the 29 ex-Luftwaffe RF-4Es, which complemented an original seven RF-4Es delivered in 1978, and serve as tactical reconnaissance platforms, replacing ageing RF-5As and RF-84F Thunderflashes. Of the Phantom units, 337 Mira (squadron) is a dedicated interceptor squadron, while 348 Mira is tasked with tactical reconnaissance. Both units are based at Larissa as part of the 110th Combat Wing. The remaining two squadrons, 338 Mira (originally an interceptor squadron) and 339 Mira (originally a ground attack squadron) have been re-designed as multi-role units. No 339 Mira also acts as the F-4 conversion unit, although Phantom conversion is made overly complex by the Hellenic Air Force requirement that every F-4 pilot must first amass 300 hours as an F-4 'backseater'. These two remaining units serve as part of the 117th Combat Wing at Andravida. Recently the HAF embarked on an internal exchange programme, which saw the ex-US ANG Hill Gray II F-4Es of 338 Mira swapped for the original batch of F-4Es with 337 Mira and vice versa.

In accordance with other Phantom operators, Greece has been actively looking to upgrade about 39 F-4Es in a similar programme to Germany's F-4F ICE examples. After a succession of bids from both Israel, United States and Germany, in August 1997 Greece announced a combined DASA/Israel Aircraft Industries team had been awarded the contract (see *Phantom Upgrades*) that will prolong the service life of the F-4s until an estimated 2015. The Hellenic Aerospace Industry is currently carrying out a structural modification extension programme on up to 70 F-4Es and RF-4Es.

Iran

Beginning in September 1968 with the delivery of 32 **F-4Ds** – supplemented by 16 **RF-4Es** in February 1971 and 177 **F-4Es** from that March – Iran quickly established itself as the second largest overseas operator of the Phantom, with 225 examples distributed among a dozen squadrons. Following the

The Luftwaffe is still a major NATO user of the F-4, with four squadrons still operational and likely to remain so for at least another decade. LUIGINO CALIARO.

CURRENT LUFTWAFFE AF UNITS			
Jadgeschwader 71 'Richtofen'	F-4F-ICE	JG71	Wittmund
Jadgeschwader 72 'Westfalen'	F-4F-ICE	JG72	Hopsten
Jadgeschwader 73 'Steinhoff'	F-4F-ICE	JG73	Laage
Jadgeschwader 74 'Molders'	F-4F-ICE	JG74	Neuberg
20th FS 'The Silver Lobos'	F-4F/F-4F-ICE	20th FS	Holloman AFB
(Jadgeschwader [JG] = fighter wings)			

down capability against multiple targets and improved beyond-visual-range targeting. Fundamental changes saw the replacement of the Westinghouse AN/APQ-120 radar by an all-digital multi-mode AN/APG-65, allowing for the capability to fire the AIM-120 AMRAAM.

Delivery of modified aircraft to front-line units began in April 1992, the ICE programme being completed in October 1996. The ICE programme will allow Luftwaffe Phantoms to remain effective within Europe until at least 2012, when it is estimated that the Eurofighter will, at last, be fully in service.

The RF-4Es were retired quickly from service following the introduction of the Tornado in the tactical reconnaissance role: the final examples served until 1994 with AG 52. For more details on German F-4s see page 56.

Greece

Serving with the Takiki Aeroporikis Dynamis (Tactical Air Force) Greece's four squadrons of

Phantoms fulfil the roles of interception, fighter-bomber and reconnaissance, comprising two wings of the 28th TAF. First delivered in 1974 under Operation PEACE ICARUS, the original batch of 56 F-4Es was supplemented in 1991 by 28

Greece has operated Phantoms since 1974, an upgrade programme was instituted in 1997. F-4E 01514 is seen taxiing at Andravida in July 1995. AFM-ALAN WARNES

The Imperial Iranian Air Force eventually received over 200 Phantoms. This aircraft is seen at Mehrabad in the early-1970s.

Islamic fundamentalist revolution, which swept the Shah from power and turned against his US backers, this was assumed by many in the West to signal the end of Phantom operations within the Islamic Republic of Iran Air Force (IRIAF). Due to heavy attrition and combat losses from its war with Iraq, Iran's current operational Phantom fleet has been significantly reduced and is estimated at no more than 30 F-4Es and six RF-4Es. The original batch of F-4Ds has been retired, their loss supplemented by the purchase of 12-16 examples from South Korea. For more details on Iranian F-4s see page 74-79.

For more details on Iranian F-4s see page 74-79.

CURRENT ISLAMIC REPUBLIC OF IRAN AF UNITS			
No 3 Tactical Air Base	F-4D/E	31TFS	Hamadan-Shahroki
No 6 Tactical Air Base	F-4D/E	32TFS	Busher
No 10 Tactical Air Base	F-4D/E	101TFS	Chabahar

Israel

Following the 1967 Six-Day War between Israel and her Arab neighbours, the United States became the largest overseas supplier of aircraft to the Israeli Air Force (Heyl HaAvir). After an initial order for 48 Douglas A-4Hs and TA-4H trainers was completed in late 1967, a contract was negotiated for the supply of 44 **F-4E** and six **RF-4E** Phantoms under Operations PEACE ECHO and PEACE PATCH, and this generated much controversy. The Israel Defence Force/Air Force (IDF/AF) received its first Phantom in September 1969. The first four aircraft were delivered to Hatzor on September 5, 1969, for a formal acceptance ceremony presided over by Prime Minister Golda Meir. These went to a newly-formed unit described in the West as 201 Sqn. One rumour suggests that these were not the first Phantoms to be delivered to Israel, since an unknown number of unmarked US Navy F-4Bs were reportedly flown to Wheelus AFB, Libya, where they were picked up by civilian Caucasian pilots and delivered eastwards during 1962. (Any further information relating to this event would be welcome - Editor).

The original F-4Es were delivered at the rate of four a month, initially without leading-edge slats and Target Identification System Electro Optical (TISEO). Sixty-eight were new-build aircraft delivered under Operation PEACE ECHO (along with six RF-4Es), and 12 more followed under Operation PEACE PATCH. Additional deliveries included a further six RF-4Es and 125 more F-4Es (sometimes quoted as 124). Six of these were new-build aircraft and

included the NICKEL GRASS delivery of aircraft, variously described as 36 or 40 ex-USAF F-4Es. Phantoms from the second batch of 24 new-build F-4Es for Israel were compatible with the AGM-78 Standard ARM. At their peak, Israeli F-4s equipped six strike squadrons (their air defence role being secondary).

Such is the volatile nature of the region that the F-4s were immediately in combat, conducting strike missions against Egyptian airfields in the so-called (undeclared) War of Attrition. SAM sites were attacked in October and on December 15, 1969, while other missions that year included a sabre-rattling supersonic run by two F-4s over Cairo on November 5 and the downing of a MiG-21 on November 11.

Operations continued at much the same pace throughout January and February the following year, although the F-4Es began to meet opposition in the form of Egyptian MiG-21s. On April 2, the first F-4E was shot down by an Egyptian MiG-21 and its crew taken prisoner. A further F-4E was lost a few days later after a mechanical failure. Sporadic attacks continued, but from March 1970, Egypt began to bring forward its SAM network towards the Suez Canal, and Phantom losses began to mount. Two were lost on June 30, and another on July 5. Two more followed on July 18, one of which killed the CO of 201 Sqn, Schmuel Hetz. Kills claimed by F-4 crews totalled eight Mirage IIIs and two MiG-21s, the latter being flown by Russian volunteers. A cease-fire ended the War of Attrition on August 7, 1971.

However, IDF/AF F-4s continued to fly combat operations, with the first AGM-45 Shrike

missile launched in September 1971. The Phantoms' kill tally continued to rise, with the destruction of two Syrian Su-7s on September 9, 1972, and four MiG-21s on January 8, 1973. A bizarre kill on February 21 saw the destruction of a Libyan Arab Airlines Boeing 727, which strayed into Israeli air space and refused to respond to repeated radio warnings.

With the outbreak of the Yom Kippur War, Israeli F-4 losses had totalled eight F-4Es – at least two being shot down. The other side of the coin showed the destruction of at least 11 enemy aircraft. The opening engagements of the war saw F-4s claim at least seven MiGs along with five Mi-8 *Hips*. The first missions against Egyptian SAM sites took place the following day, an ill-planned attack which saw the destruction of six F-4s, with two crews killed and the rest captured. A further F-4E was downed on an undisclosed mission on October 8. Further losses occurred the following day, with attacks against Egyptian airfields. One aircraft was lost, while another F-4 managed to recover to an IDF/AF base with several 57mm hits. Attacks continued throughout the following months, the ever-increasing SAM threat claiming many F-4s before a change in tactics allowed Phantom crews to conduct combined low-level strikes against the sites. Losses to MiGs were mainly a result of heavily-laden F-4s being ambushed on route to their targets, but at no time did the

CURRENT IDF/AF UNITS			
Bacha 8	F-4E-2000/RF-4E	119 Sqn 'Bat'	Tel Nov
	F-4E-2000/RF-4E	201 Sqn 'Ahat'	Tel Nov
(Bacha = Wing)			

Israel has had the longest combat record with the F-4, aircraft taking part in a number of conflicts with Arab states. ISRAEL AIRCRAFT INDUSTRIES

Japan is the only country to have licence-built the F-4, as the F-4EJ; the Phantom remains a key part of the JASDF, with over 100 aircraft still in service. KATSUHIKO TOKUNAGA

Egyptian pilots prove superior to the crews of the F-4s. By the end of the war, 37 Phantoms had been lost and six more were so badly damaged they had to be written off. The losses were made good by the transfer of 36 (or 40) USAF examples during Operation NICKEL GRASS.

Following their extensive combat history, all of Israel's F-4 fleet received battle damage of some kind during the Yom Kippur War. The urgent need to repair the aircraft was paralleled by the requirement to update the Phantom's avionics and weapons delivery systems, and to add slats to any remaining aircraft. Most Israeli F-4s have an Elbit Jason digital weapons system, and some have strap-on in-flight refuelling probes. A Cathode Ray Tube (CRT) is provided for the navigator. A number of optional electro-optical/FLIR systems were also evaluated for the Phantoms.

Since the end of the war, Israeli F-4s have continued to fly combat missions, this time against the PLO in the 1982 Lebanon War. One Egyptian MiG-21 was claimed on December 6, 1973, while two F-4Es were shot down in April 1974. During this time, F-4s were operating exclusively in the air-to-ground role, having lost their interceptor role to newly-delivered F-15 Eagles. The final Phantom air-to-air kill was claimed on June 11, 1982, with the downing of a Syrian MiG-21 using a Rafael Python over the Bekaa Valley – the 116th F-4 kill.

Such is the importance of the F-4 within the IDF/AF that a further upgrade was undertaken for 55 of the remaining 97 aircraft. Known as the Kurnass 2000, it involved both structural/avionics improvements and a modernised instrument layout and wide-angle head-up display. Kurnass 2000s entered service in 1989. While the exploits of the F-4Es are widely known, those of the RF-4E fleet

are still the subject of debate and rumour. What is known is that three examples were covertly modified by General Dynamics (now Lockheed Martin) in 1975-76. The programme saw the addition of a HIAC-1 long-range oblique optical camera (LOROP) system. Designated as F-4ES (Special), the remaining two examples (one having been shot down in 1982) serve alongside other RF-4Es at Tel Nov, though recent speculation seems to confirm that reconnaissance-configured RF-4s are spread amongst the F-4E fighter-bomber units, of which there are three remaining. Within Israel, RF-4s are known as Orefs (Ravens). Of these squadrons, 119, 142 and 201, all operate F-4E-2000s. With other upgrades planned, Israeli F-4s look set to continue in service for at least the next ten years, although the recently announced acquisition of 50 F-16s with an option for another 60 could hinder such prospects. For more details on Israel Phantoms see page 48-52

Japan

The only Phantoms not built by the parent company at St Louis were those manufactured under licence in Japan by Mitsubishi. After the ending of prohibition of Japanese military forces in 1954, the Koku Jiei Tai (Japanese Air Self-Defence Force - JASDF) was established almost exclusively with American-built aircraft. But as the nation's manufacturing industries were rebuilt, greater emphasis came to be laid on licence production of foreign aircraft, and during the Third Defence Build-up Programme (DBP) of 1965-70, it was decided to negotiate licence production of the F-4 Phantom.

Two pattern **F-4EJ** prototypes were built by McDonnell Douglas and delivered in July 1971. McDonnell Douglas also supplied Mitsubishi with 11 kits of parts and two forward fuselages.

The first Japanese-assembled aircraft, (there would eventually be 130) flew on May 27, 1972, and the last, was delivered to the JASDF on May 20, 1981, this latter also having the distinction of being the last Phantom II built. In addition, 14 RF-4EJs were supplied from US production runs, delivery taking place between June 1974 and November 1975. The F-4EJs entered service with 301, 302, 303 and 304 Squadrons of the 8th Air Wing based at Hyakuri, Chitose and Tsuiki. Ten further aircraft ordered in 1977 served with 305 Squadron. With the final example in service, Japan immediately undertook an upgrade programme which saw the incorporation of a new APG-66J

F-4EJ

Optimised for the air defence role, this Japanese version of the F-4E dispensed with the AN/AJB-7 bombing system and had no provision for air-to-ground conventional and special weapons. It was fitted with a data link system with the Japanese BADGE (Base Air Defence Ground Environment) system and Japanese J/APR-2 tail warning radar. As built, the Japanese F-4EJs were not fitted with an in-flight refuelling receptacle, but this was retrofitted. Whereas the retrofit of leading edge slats was considered but not implemented, the Japanese later approved the replacement of the APQ-120 radar with an APG-66J.

CURRENT JASDF UNITS

3rd Kokudan	F-4EJ-Kai	8 Hikotai	Misawa
5th Kokudan	F-4EJ-Kai/ F-4EJ	301 Hikotai	Nyutabaru
83th Kokugun	F-4EJ-Kai/ F-4EJ	302 Hikotai	Naha
Direct Reporting Units	RF-4E/ RF-4E-Kai/ RF-4EJ	501 Hikotai	Hyakuri

(Kokudan = Air Wing, Kokugun = Air Group, Hikotai = Squadron)

radar able to operate in the look-down/shoot-down mode with the emerging new generation of Air to Air missiles (AAMs). The 90 upgraded aircraft were designated F-4EJ Kai – (Kai meaning 'modified').

Alongside the interceptors, the remaining 12 of an original 14 **RF-4Es** were also upgraded with forward-looking radar and ELINT pods. The introduction of the F-15EJ has seen the Phantom fleet dwindle, but over 100 F-4EJs are still in service, now split between two interceptor-fighter units located at Nytabaru AB (Dai 301 Hikotai) and in the south-west at Naha AB (Dai 302 Hikotai); the single fighter support (FS) squadron, Dai 8 Hikotai, is at Misawa AB. Each squadron is equipped with a number of unmodified F-4EJs for training/support tasks, such as target towing. Providing Japan's tactical reconnaissance is one squadron of RF-4EJs serving with Dai 501 Hikotai at Hyakuri AB, consisting of RF-4E/RF-4E Kais and 17 former F-4EJs converted to RF-4Es, though further examples may be converted. For more details on Japanese F-4s see *Air Forces Monthly*, March 00, p78-82

South Korea

Since the end of the Korean War in 1953, relations between North and South Korea have remained volatile, with the result that the United States has continued to assist in the strengthening of the Republic of Korea Air Force (RoKAF). In 1969, 18 **F-4Ds** began to replace F-86s then in service with the RoKAF's 1st Fighter Wing, and in 1972 – after South Korean F-5s were transferred to South Vietnam – a further batch of 18 F-4Ds was supplied. In 1977, 30 **F-4Es**, together with 341 AIM-7E Sparrow AAMs, were delivered to complete the equipping of four squadrons, under the PEACE PHEASANT II programme, the first delivery of F-4Ds being titled PEACE PHEASANT I. Early model Phantoms continue to equip the 110th TFS at Taegu, whilst the F-4Es are split between two Chongju units, the 152nd TFS and 153rd TFS.

Phantoms reached their peak strength in the 1980s with a total of 71 F-4Ds and 55 F-4Es in service, along with 18 RF-4Cs of the 131st TRS at Suwon. The RoKAF has made a number of proposals to upgrade its F-4 fleet, work earmarked to be undertaken by Boeing. However, the recent downturn in the regional economy has curtailed any such plans at present.

CURRENT SOUTH KOREAN AF UNITS

11th Tactical Air Wing	F-4D	110th TFS	Taegu
	F-4D	151st TFS	Taegu
17th Tactical Air Wing	F-4E	132nd TFS	Chongju
	F-4E	152nd TFS	Chongju
	F-4E	153rd TFS	Chongju
39th Tactical Reconnaissance Group	RF-4C	131st TRS	Suwon

Spain

Spain's first introduction to the Phantom came in 1972 when 36 ex-USAF **F-4Cs** were delivered to two Escuadrons (squadrons), 121 and 122 as part of Ala 12 (12th Wing), which was in the process of replacing F-86F Sabres and F-104G Starfighters. Serving in the interception role, the F-4Cs fulfilled Spain's QRA role armed with AIM-9J Sidewinders, AIM-7E Sparrows and 20mm gunpods. The Phantoms were withdrawn from service in April

Phantoms replaced F-86s with the RoKAF in 1969; today it operates approximately 60 F-4Es flying with 11 Wing at Taegu and the 17th Wing at Chongju. This example wears the marks of 153 'Bear' Squadron. JIM WALG

1979 following the arrival of EF-18A/B Hornets. However, this was not to be the end of the Phantom in Spanish skies – eight **RF-4Cs** purchased from ex-USAF ANG stocks arrived in January 1989. Designated the CR.12 within Spanish squadrons, the RF-4s serve with Escuadron 123 of Ala 12, based at Tarragon de Ardoz.

An effort to increase the reconnaissance fleet by acquiring ex-Luftwaffe RF-4Es came to nothing. A limited upgrade has been made to the fleet by the introduction of terrain following radar, new ECM systems and electro-optical sensors and real-time data-links, and this will allow the aircraft to remain in service for at least the next five to six years. For more details of Spanish F-4s, see page 26.

CURRENT SPANISH AF UNITS

Ala 12	RF-4C
123 Escuadron	Torrejon

Turkey

Turkey became a major Phantom operator in 1973, deliveries of 40 F-4Es taking place under the PEACE DIAMOND III. Operators included 161 Filo (squadron) of 6 Ana Jet US. In 1977, a further order comprised 32 more F-4Es and eight **RF-4Es**. These aircraft equipped three squadrons, replacing the F-100 Super Sabre and RF-5As of Eskishehir's 1st JAB – 111, 112 and 113 Squadrons. One F-4E delivered to the Turk Hava Kuvvetleri (Turkish Air Force) was the 5,000th example produced at St Louis. Several batches of former USAF F-4Es have subsequently been obtained in order to convert two more Squadrons – 131 and 132. These batches comprised 15 from June 1981; 15 in mid-1984; 15 in 1986 and 40 in June-

October 1987. As recognition for Turkish support of UN forces in the 1991 Gulf War, 40 more were delivered in March 1991. Thus, the final figure for F-4s is about 205. Turkish F-4s are undergoing an upgrade, the work being performed by IAI Lahav Division, with 54 examples to be brought up to Phantom 2000 standard. These modifications will see Turkish F-4s in service for the next 15 to 20 years. The first two to be completed were redelivered to Turkey on January 21, 2000 and formally handed over six days later. For more details on Turkish F-4s see page 38.

United States Civilian Operations

Though no longer in service with any of America's armed forces, Phantoms continue to fly in US skies as pilotless airborne targets for the emerging new generation of AAMs. With a requirement for at least 300 **QF-4E/G** drones, Tracor Systems of Austin, Texas, is undertaking these conversions where the aircraft are operated by 82 Aerial Targets Squadron at Tyndall AFB, Florida. The US Navy Naval Weapons Test Center (USN NWTC) at NAS Point Mugu, California, also finds use for the former – its vast fleet of tired Phantoms for weapons trials platforms with 14 **QF-4Ns** is the first of many more **QF-4S** conversions now taking place. For more details see pages 32-35 and page 45-47.

CURRENT US MILITARY OPERATORS

82nd Aerial Targets Squadron	QF-4E/QF-4G	Tyndall AFB, FL
82nd ATS Det 1	QF-4E/QF-4G	Holloman AFB, MN
US Navy Naval Weapons Test Center	QF-4N/QF-4S	NAS Point Mugu, CA

CURRENT TURKISH AF UNITS

1AJU	F-4E	111 Filo 'Panter' (Panther)	Eskisehir		Bomber
	F-4E	112 Filo 'Seytan' (Devil)	Eskisehir		Air Defence
	RF-4E	113 Filo 'Isik' (Light)	Eskisehir		Recce
7AJU	F-4E	171 Filo 'Korsan' (Buccaneer)	Erhac-Malataya		Bomber
	F-4E	172 Filo 'Sahin' (Falcon)	Erhac-Malataya		Air Defence
	RF-4E	173 Filo 'Safak' (Dawn)	Erhac-Malataya		Recce
3AJU	F-4E	131 Filo 'Ejder' (Dragon)	Konya		Combat Readiness Training
	F-4E	132 Filo 'Haner' (Dagger)	Konya		Weapons/Tactics Training
(AJU = Ana Jet Us Komutanlg – Main Jet Base)					

Bear Hunting

Tony Dixon, a navigator on RAF Phantoms for seven years in the 1980s, discusses the aircraft's Air Defence role.

THE PARTY IS in full swing. The beautiful blonde across the room smiles and walks towards you. As she gets close to you, she whispers in your ear..............

............"NORTHERN Q to cockpit readiness!"

The words come out of the small box by your bed – the Telebrief, a semi-secure line to the Sector Operations Centre at RAF Buchan, near Aberdeen.

The sheets are thrown back from the bed as you grope for the light switch, pulling on your 'bunny' suit for thermal insulation. Next comes the immersion suit (no time for G pants, provided you remembered to put a bung in the hole in the immersion suit that the G pant hose normally fits) carefully pulling the rubber seals over your head and wrists as the last thing you need at – I wonder what time it is anyway, it's still dark outside – is to rip the seal. Pull on the flying boots, using the zips (great US modification – saves time with the laces), run for the door,. picking up your watch (3 am, nice!) while bumping into your crewie and then the two members of Q2 in the corridor to the Q-shed. The navigator hits the button to open the doors and starts the Houchin (unless the groundcrew are already there). Run to the bottom of the ladder, grab your Mae West, donning it while trying to climb the ladder at the same time. Jump into your seat still pulling on your helmet, and start to strap in. Connect your Personal Equipment Connector (PEC) and establish comms with Buchan.

"41 Cockpit Ready" you lie, still trying to strap in. At least you have beaten Q2, as they transmit about five seconds later. The pilot has already started the starboard engine as you wave away the groundcrew, who remove the ladder so that the left can be started.

"41 Vector 340 Climb Flight Level 250 for Buchan control TAD 26 backup 59, Scramble, Scramble, Scramble acknowledge!"

"340, 250 26 backup 59,41 Scrambles."

The pilot waves away the chocks as you both finish strapping in. Don't forget the Dinghy connection and Leg Restraints. A quick "ready" from you and he increases the power to get the beast moving. The Telebrief disconnects as the aircraft moves and you establish comms with the tower. They are as awake as you are as the Telebrief has roused them from slumber as well, and as you taxi several people are checking lights, runway clearance, the fire section and radios.

"41 Taxy"

"41 Taxy, runway 27, QFE 1020, Wind Velocity 260 degrees 15 knots."

Blast! Too much of a tailwind for 09, and therefore a two-mile taxy to get to the end of 27. (The QRA sheds at RAF Leuchars prior to the construction of the Hardened Aircraft Shelters [HAS] were at the western end of the airfield.) That will delay our take–off by a couple of minutes and so increase the response time. A maximum of ten minutes is allowed, but every scramble is measured for the exact time. Pre-takeoff checks are read challenge and response so that everything is finished prior to the holding point.

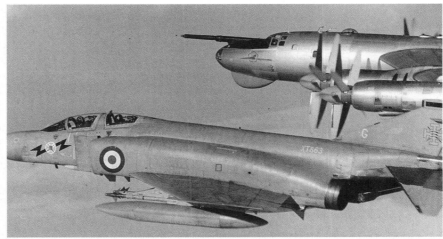

Tu-95MS Bear-H strategic bombers were once regularly intercepted by F-4 Phantoms, but now this task is undertaken by the type's air defence successor, the Tornado F.3 COLIN FRYER

"41 Takeoff."

"41 clear takeoff surface wind 250/15."

The aircraft moves onto the runway centreline. Full power – rock outboard – full reheat. Three seconds later the power of the Rolls-Royce engines bites. The ground roll is longer than normal, with three external tanks and eight missiles, but 30 seconds later the inhabitants of Balmullo are wakened.

The village is about two-thirds of a mile from the end of the runway and has been enlarged by a new housing estate, built when the Leuchars runway was being resurfaced, hence no noisy aircraft. The aircraft turns onto its northerly heading and climbs to its assigned altitude. A quick call to Scottish Air Traffic clears us through the airway before contacting Buchan on prebrief...

History

Re-equipped with the Phantom FG.1 at RAF Leuchars on September 1, 1969, 43 Squadron took a short time to adapt the F-4 to United Kingdom Air Defence Region (UKADR) procedures and it was not until July 1, 1970 that the squadron was declared operational on type. The advantages gained by the extra range, increased firepower and improved radar performance gave the Phantom a superior ability over the Lightning. (The latter, of course, was a superb aircraft that, if fought to its own rules, could defeat the F-4, but on paper and with practice the F-4 crews would invariably beat the Lightning pilots.) When 111 Squadron re-formed with the Phantom FGR.2 at Leuchars on November 3, 1975, the base became the home of Phantom Northern QRA. As the Royal Navy started to get rid of its F-4s, the RAF decided to make Leuchars a Phantom FG.1 wing. 'Treble One' therefore lost its Inertial Navigation System (INS) and High Frequency (HF) long-range radio equipped aircraft and instead operated the FG.1 with a normal V/UHF radio and a navigation system (Air Position Indicator) that, at best, was untrustworthy and, at worst, was completely useless! How the Royal Navy crews ever found their ships is a complete mystery if the TACAN (the only true navigational aid on the aircraft) was not working.

Phantom FG.1

The Naval version, the F-4K, known in the UK as the FG.1, maintained the ability to carry four

Above: *Prior to Hardened Aircraft Shelters being built at Leuchars, aircraft were sometimes left outside overnight to suffer the Scottish weather.*

Right: *Red tails were painted on some aircraft to assist with identification during in-close combat situations. Serial number XV420 was the personal mount of 56 Squadron boss Barry Titchen, and is seen cleaning up following a pairs take-off at RAF Leuchars.*

Below: *The unofficial QRA in Cyprus sometimes caught 'different' intercepts. This Israeli F-4 was on an air test to the south of the island.*

AIM-7 Sparrow/ BAe Skyflash and four AIM-9 Sidewinder missiles. The navigator controlled the intercept using the AN/AWG 10/11 radar, capable of picking up contacts well in excess of 50 nm (80 km), and once in a firing position, the pilot pulled the trigger and fired the missile. The aircraft could also carry the SUU-23 six-barrel Gatling gun capable of firing an astonishing 100 rounds a second! TACAN provided the only efficient piece of navigation kit with a maximum range of 200 nm, but the radar could also be used with ground returns being visible in excess of 150 nm. A later modification to the aircraft was TESS – basically a Chieftain tank gunsight. A low-power telescope, fixed to the centreline of the aircraft and depressed two degrees, was attached to the left-hand side of the aircraft. Once the navigator had the contact on radar, the pilot selected radar boresight. This was linked to the head-up display (HUD) and all the pilot needed to do was, once visual, point at the target at range. The navigator then looked

through the TESS, giving an identification of the target at around 10 nm head-on on a fighter-sized target.

Power was provided by two Rolls-Royce Spey 203 turbofans, one of which was mounted upside-down to fit into the space available! (Reading the oil level was achieved with an extendable mirror and a torch!) These engines had a fast reheat capability to ease 'bolters' on a carrier, but this facility was inhibited in RAF service and the reheats could take up to three seconds to 'bite'. The aircraft was started by an external power source, as it did not have an internal battery. Despite all its problems, the aircraft was liked by its operators and respected by its adversaries.

Quick Reaction Alert (QRA)

Until the mid-1980s, Northern and Southern QRA defended the UKADR, Northern Q being at Leuchars and Southern Q alternating between Binbrook, Coningsby and Wattisham, until the Tornado F3 era when Leeming also became a

QRA base. Each squadron would take a three-week stint of Q, which meant a Southern Q squadron would be 'on' for three weeks in every four-and-a-half months! Northern Q was three weeks on, three weeks off, three weeks on, three weeks off, etc, for 365 days a year. The duty squadron provided two aircraft on ten-minute readiness at the Q sheds 24 hours a day, seven days a week, with a third aircraft to be ready within 60 minutes if necessary. Two full crews spent 24 hours on duty with a third crew on call. If Q was launched, which was not an uncommon occurrence, the third crew was called in.

Normal procedure was that both aircraft would start engines but only Q1 would launch. Q2 would remain at cockpit until Q1 was declared serviceable. (The Americans on Iceland used to launch both QRA aircraft following an incident where an F-4 had been lost in mysterious circumstances during an intercept.) If Buchan considered that the 'X-Ray' or 'Zombie', the unidentified track that Q

had been launched to intercept, was going to remain in the UKADR, the option was available to launch a tanker aircraft, the idea being either to rendezvous with Q1 to refuel or to pick up Q2 as it passed Leuchars, or even to bring Southern Q1 north to give the southern squadrons some trade. The tankers were either Victors from Marham, Vulcans from Waddington, or VC-10s from Brize Norton.

Multiple Zombies often required multiple Q aircraft and it was not unknown to get many Leuchars aircraft airborne and Southern Q as well, especially if there was a large naval exercise to the north of the UK. Help was then required from the other squadrons to provide relief crews as aircrew were only allowed to fly for seven hours before being replaced. Engineers would also be working overtime generating the extra armed aircraft.

Once north of the Scottish mainland, an update on the 'traffic' was requested. If the scramble had been no-notice, as in the example at the start of this article, the crews

literally had no idea of what to expect. It was then up to Buchan to relay track information with regard to strength, height, speed and any other known information. Slow speed low or medium level contacts were invariably Ilyushin *Coots* or *Mays*. High level were Tupolev *Bears*, *Badgers*, or very rarely Myasischev *Bisons*. Passing Saxa Vord, the work started in earnest. Ground radar contact on the traffic would have been lost as they left Norwegian airspace and the F104s or F16s of the Norwegian Air Force would have gone home (no air-to-air refuelling for them!). Intelligence sources would provide Buchan with some information, but it was really up to the Phantom navigator to earn his pay. Occasionally it would be the pilot who would get a visual – at a range of about 80 nm. (It is very difficult to hide if the aircraft is contrailing!) Interception on a pair would start with the rear aircraft as you can always see what the leader is doing. Once the identification had been made – usually from the serial on the nose-wheel door – and a couple of photographs taken, a second intercept would be made on the leader. Even in the cockpit of the F-4, it was possible to hear the noise of the Kuznetsov engines from a *Bear*. The aircraft would then be shadowed until they left the UKADR or it was time for tanking. A clever tanker captain would also be shadowing the *Bears* in about three miles (4.82km) trail so that the contacts would not be lost while the F-4 topped up its tanks. *Bear* Foxtrots would sometimes require a little more work by the intercepting, as their operating area was low-level in their submarine hunter role. You just had to make sure that your aircraft was not sitting on the inside wingtip in a low-level turn, or even directly behind as the aircraft was laying Sonabuoys!

Eventually, the traffic would turn for home, but the F-4 would remain on Combat Air Patrol (CAP) for some 10-15 minutes just to make sure before returning to Leuchars. Once back

Above: *Short notice missile firings also kept the QRA crews awake. Sometimes however, a particular variant of missile was required, so a non-Q aircraft was used. XV574/Z is seen with a single Sparrow.*
Left: *Arguably the best modern fighter in the RAF, the F-4J(UK) flew mostly with a single centreline tank or in the clean configuration. Note the 'strap-on' refuelling probe, as opposed to the FG.1 and FGR.2, and the different engine nozzles from the J79 engines.*

A pleasant day in the Falklands. QRA aircraft in the South Atlantic fly daily to keep the aircraft and the crews current. AFM FILES

in the Q-shed, the engineers would refuel the aircraft while the crew made out a mission report and grabbed a coffee and something to eat before putting the aircraft back 'on-state' ready for the next scramble.

Germany

In the 1960s and 1970s the Lightning, from its base in Gutersloh, had been responsible for the RAF's part in the air defence of the former West Germany. When it was superseded by the Phantom in 1975, the operating base was changed to Wildenrath on the Dutch border and another 100 miles (160km) from the Air Defence Identification Zone (ADIZ). However, the reaction time of only **five** minutes was not altered. From Gutersloh, which is only a couple of minutes flying time from the ADIZ, the reaction time had some relevance, but from Wildenrath, 20 minutes flying time to the border, a five-minute state was a little optimistic. However, the F-4 maintained this readiness throughout its operations from Wildenrath. Here, QRA was conducted differently from the way it was conducted in the UK: each Squadron, 19 and 92, held one aircraft and crew at 24-hour readiness in a separate Hardened Aircraft Shelter (HAS) on opposite sides of the taxiway. Although the aircrew did not have to wear immersion suits as they did in the UK, there was no time to dress if a scramble occurred at night, so you lived and slept in your flying suit. Also, the first crew to check in at cockpit got the scramble. This led, not surprisingly, to a good deal of inter-squadron rivalry! Although scrambles were relatively common, they were mainly to exercise the system (and check the response times). Some 'real' intercepts were made, but these were mainly on private pilots unsure of position. By the time the Phantoms reached the ADIZ, the target aircraft had either found itself or landed.

There were instances of Eastern Bloc aircraft infringing the area, normally cutting across parts of West Germany that stuck out into the East. These infringements lasted a matter of seconds

and therefore were extremely difficult, if not impossible, to intercept. The Phantoms used in Germany were the F-4M/ FGR.2 with INS, which took 105 seconds minimum for full use from turning on to taxy. The fact that they still achieved scramble times of less than five minutes to airborne shows how good the crews were.

Cyprus

Once every 12 to 18 months, each Air Defence (AD) squadron spent four weeks at RAF Akrotiri in Cyprus on Armament Practice Camp (APC)

to qualify to the NATO standard in air-to-air gunnery. It was not uncommon for a spare aircraft to be held on unofficial QRA in case of any unidentified tracks around the southern part of the island. Syrian Tupolev Tu-16 Badgers routinely flew patrols in the area, plus occasional Ilyushin Il-18 Coots or Il-38 Mays. Other countries bordering the eastern Mediterranean also used the airspace for training and their aircraft were sometimes encountered. 'Real' QRA was mounted during Operation PULSATOR – the Lebanese crisis – when RAF Buccaneers from Akrotiri flew

Above: *Until recently, the only form of method in the Falklands utilised the Hercules. Again a single hose and a stable basket –the Rolls-Royce Spey engines on the F-4 allowed better performance at slow speed.*
Right: *The power of the 'Mighty Phantom' is demonstrated by this 1435 Flight FGR.2 over the Falkland Islands. Note that only two Skyflash missiles were carried to reduce wear on the fins, and an SUU-23 six-barrel Gatling gun is mounted instead of the extra fuel tank.*
Below: *QRA, or 'Battle Flight' as it was better known in Germany, had to cross most of western Germany before any intercept could be made. Training sorties used the low-flying areas to famil-iarise the crews with the terrain.* PHOTOS, AUTHOR UNLESS STATED

missions over the Lebanon. RAF Phantoms provided top cover for those missions, and 24-hour defence of the British forces on the island.

Falkland Islands

During the Falklands War, Phantoms from 29 Squadron patrolled the skies around Ascension Island in the middle of the Atlantic Ocean. Ascension was the main staging post for supplying the Task Force before it sailed south. Once the war had been fought, work was done on the airfield at Port Stanley to enable the Phantoms to operate from the islands. This included the laying of a metal 'mat' to extend the runway, and the installation of five Arrestor cables to enable the aircraft to stop. At just over 4,000 ft (1,200m), a normal landing for the F-4 was ill-advised! The first aircraft, still from 29 Squadron, arrived at Stanley on October 17, 1982. No 23 squadron from Wattisham replaced 29 in December before the task was shared between all squadrons in February 1983, though the name remained as 23 Squadron, and the unit callsign has been 'The Eagles' ever since. A normal 'tour' lasted four months, later being reduced to five weeks following the move to RAF Mount Pleasant in early 1986.

Two aircraft were maintained on QRA at a ten-minute readiness, 24 hours a day. There were no shelters for these aircraft as the only hangars were of the semi-portable type that consisted of an tubular aluminium frame over which was stretched a waterproof covering to keep out the elements. There was a maximum wind speed limit for opening the doors of these hangarettes and so the Q aircraft were kept outside in case they were needed to scramble when the wind was too strong to open the doors! To keep the number of crews in the Falklands to a minimum, a crew was on call (either as Q1 or Q2 in the 'shed', or Q3 on call

in the 'Mess'. The latter was initially a converted cruise ship, then eventually a Coastel, which was normally used for oilrig workers, consisting of a collection of containers joined together, with living accommodation inside. With the uncertainty of the Argentinian intention, tension was high in the early days of the Falklands. Work had started on the new airport some 20 miles (32km) away at Mount Pleasant. The runway was opened in 1985, enabling airborne resupply and remanning, but the 'Phandet' did not move in to its new accommodation until May 1986. Mount Pleasant 'normalised' QRA with more permanent hangars, although the wind could still be a problem. If there was a strong westerly wind blowing, it was impossible to walk through the tunnel to the Q1 shed because of the funnelling effect of the wind. Instead you had to climb over the revetment around the hangar to get to your aircraft! Scrambles were reasonably frequent as there was (and still is) some dispute as to the airspace and sea areas surrounding the Islands. Intercepted aircraft include Argentinian Navy Electras, Fokker F28s and very occasionally the ELINT Boeing 707s. Any aircraft approaching the Islands was intercepted, including the RAF Tristars, British Airways Boeing 747s which were used before the RAF Tristars were in use, and Britannia Airways Boeing 767s, used when the Tristars were undergoing servicing following the Gulf War.

In November 1987, 23 Squadron was named 1435 Flight, shrinking from its seven aircraft to just four. As the Flight had served on Malta during World War Two, the Falklands aircraft were called Faith, Hope and Charity (after the Gloster Gladiators that defended the Mediterranean Island)– with Desperation thrown in for good measure. Although Mount Pleasant has a shorter secondary runway to

cope for the strong winds common to the South Atlantic, aircraft operations have to keep a good eye on the sometimes unpredictable weather. QRA is often 'mandatory' when the wind is high or the snow is falling, meaning that there would be a risk to aircraft and aircrew if launched. (A peculiar fact about the Falklands is that it is possible to have snow in every month of the year.) Phantoms patrolled the skies above and around the Falklands until July 1992, when Tornado F3s from the UK arrived. Three of the F4s were scrapped, while the other (XV409 – Hope) is on guard outside the air terminal.

Final Southern QRA

As the Phantom was phased out, the final outpost was RAF Wattisham in Suffolk. No 56 Squadron with FGR.2s, and No 74 (F) 'Tiger' Squadron initially with the F-4J(UK), which was replaced early in 1991 by FGR.2s. Both Squadrons undertook QRA in rotation sharing with the Tornado, until August 1990 when the Tornado held full-time QRA, and the era of the RAF F-4 Phantom defending any airspace worldwide came to an end.

So, to return to the scramble at the start of the article:

….the QRA mission did not result in an intercept. The tracks had turned back north and Q1 had been recalled to base. Leuchars at 4am in the winter is a cold, quiet place, and after the aircraft had been refuelled, the mission report filed, and a quick cup of tea drunk, the crew gets back into the aircraft to declare it 'on-state.' There is then just enough time to get a couple of hours rest before the new crews take over at 8 am.

........Great, the party's still in full swing – now where is that blonde?........

Phantom Phixers
an Armourers Perspective

In the spring of 1972 Pete Shaw met up with 'the Beast', an awesome-looking weapons platform known as the McDonnell Phantom II.

I WAS JUST 18 years old when I received my overseas posting to 14 Squadron, RAF Bruggen, West Germany – only the year previous, I had passed out from a Halton apprenticeship as a Junior Technician in the trade of Aircraft Fitter Weapons – known by other trades as Armourers or 'Plummers'.

Upon joining the squadron, I was immediately taken aback by the sheer quantity of serviceable Phantoms lined up on the pan each morning. We shared the huge concrete facility with our close neighbours, 17 Squadron, and, when both our combined jets were standing there, line abreast, it was a very impressive sight. Bruggen was also home to another Phantom squadron – No. 31, whose facilities were at the far end of the airfield and who were usually considered the poor relations to the two 'central' squadrons, for no other reason than their remoteness. Having been posted onto type with no 'conversion course' I had to learn about the Phantom as I went along, and my tasks alternated between 'First Line' and 'Second Line' (Hangar Rectification).

Hard work

This was an aircraft that required considerable hard work and many man-hours from all the trades to keep it in the air – as armourers we were kept particularly busy. Usually, whatever the unserviceability, our trade would be required to remove some piece of armament 'kit' to facilitate access to other equipment. Ejection seats were favourite – maybe the Inertial Nav/Attack System (INAS) needed replacing yet again, or perhaps one of the aircrew had dropped his pen on the previous sortie – such items could work their way into a dark crevice in the lower cockpit, requiring a full Foreign Object Deposit (FOD) search. A couple of 'plummers' could often be found hanging upside down in the front or rear cockpit, disarming and disconnecting the seats. Work on the underbelly might necessitate the removal of the Sergeant Fletcher tank from the outboard stations, the inner pylons for the benefit of the 'sparkies' or maybe the LAU 7A launcher and centreline bomb rack which would enable the 'sooties' to change the engine.

Many underbelly tasks required the armourer to move around the concrete floor on his knees, then stretching up through a very small access panel, with wrists twisted into unnatural contortions, whilst attempting to turn a spanner with his finger-tips.

Invariably, said spanner would slip off the bolt and come crashing down on the armourer's nose! But by far the worst aspect was the constant kneeling – whether it was working 'second line' or just re-arming on a 'first line' turn-round. At one time we were issued with miners' knee pads – thick rubber pads held on by straps around the leg. One task that was particularly hard on the knees was re-arming the external centreline gun pod, the SUU 23A. This was a marvellous bit of kit – when it was working properly. It consisted of a rotary cannon, with six barrels spinning at incredible speed and capable of firing around 100 rounds of 20mm ammunition per second. Problems with the gun usually stemmed from the electronic control pack which necessitated regular visits from a member of the newly-formed trade of Armament Electricians. He would plug his test box into the rear of the pod, and hopefully tell us what was wrong and that he could fix it. Otherwise the armourers would have to download all the ammunition and remove the pod from the aircraft for return to the Rectification Bay.

Before long, I was selected to undergo training as a member of a Special Weapon Load Team

Left: *This was an aircraft that required considerable hard work and many man-hours from all the trades to keep it in the air – as armourers we were kept particularly busy. Phantoms of 14 Squadron pose by one of the 'picture book' castles of Germany.* AUTHOR

Right: *Loading the SUU 23A rotary cannon could be back-breaking stuff!* AFM-DUNCAN CUBITT

Below: *The SUU 23A was a marvellous bit of kit – when it was working properly. Here an armourer gets to work on rectifying another problem.* RAF

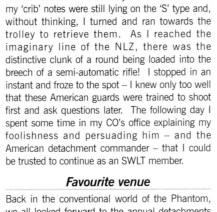

(SWLT). This involved a group of 'plummers' loading a Special Weapon (nuclear) onto the Phantom's centreline bomb station. The training was carried out using dummy concrete 'shapes' under instruction from the SWLT Training Cell. Once an acceptable standard had been reached, our team would carry out a 'certification load' which, when successfully completed, would enable us to load real 'nukes' to the aircraft in the Quick Reaction Alert (QRA) compound on the far side of the runway. This very secure area was guarded by a mix of American soldiers (the weapons were American and so American servicemen were involved in every aspect of their handling and protection) and RAF Policemen, both carrying small arms with live ammunition.

Prior to the loading, an 'S' type trolley carrying two 'nukes' would arrive on site under armed convoy and a secure sub area known as the 'No Lone Zone' would be established around the 'S' type and the aircraft to be loaded. No one was allowed within this area alone, there always had to be at least two appropriate personnel present – i.e from the loading team, aircrew or duty groundcrew.

I will always remember the completion of my first 'live' load. My team and I were walking away from the 'No Lone Zone' feeling quite pleased with ourselves, everything having gone particularly well on this occasion – suddenly I remembered that my 'crib' notes were still lying on the 'S' type and, without thinking, I turned and ran towards the trolley to retrieve them. As I reached the imaginary line of the NLZ, there was the distinctive clunk of a round being loaded into the breech of a semi-automatic rifle! I stopped in an instant and froze to the spot – I knew only too well that these American guards were trained to shoot first and ask questions later. The following day I spent some time in my CO's office explaining my foolishness and persuading him – and the American detachment commander – that I could be trusted to continue as an SWLT member.

Favourite venue

Back in the conventional world of the Phantom, we all looked forward to the annual detachments to warmer climates. Decimomannu was the NATO Armament Practice Camp (APC) in Sardinia where aircrew were given the opportunity to display their prowess in firing live rounds and dropping bombs. We groundcrew had to settle for a nice suntan and some great wine to wash down the squid rings down at Smokey Joe's hut, just outside the camp. RAF Akrotiri was also high on our list of Phantom 'phixers' favourite venues for an APC.

It was on one of the 'Deci' trips that I and three

fellow 'phixers' managed to secure back-seat sorties in the Phantom. It was a great thrill to fly in the aircraft that I had spent many long hours fixing in order that others could fly it (and very often return it broken again!). My 'driver' for this air experience flight was Flt Lt Mike Brown, whilst my best mate, Kev Connor, was to be chauffeured by Flt Lt Paul Day – well known to many these days for his work with the Battle of Britain Memorial Flight.

Another annual APC took place at RAF Valley in Anglesey, usually in atrocious weather conditions, where selected aircrews were able to chase a Jindivik drone around the sky and fire an AIM 7 Sparrow missile at it. Endless hours were spent waiting around for the weather conditions to improve long enough for the aircraft to get a 'slot'. During this 'downtime' we groundcrew honed our expertise at 'Uckers' a version of Ludo, using a homemade board and a lot of brightly painted 201 cartridges (used ones of course).

Other diversions from the routine consisted of station exercises (Minevals) and the annual Taceval, whereupon we moved our aircraft and kit to revetments located around the airfield, working long shifts to achieve our war role targets, but enjoying some great food cooked up in the field kitchens. This was in the days before the Hardened Aircraft Shelters (HAS) were built at Bruggen – the first ones being completed around the end of 1974.

After two and a half years on the 'beast', my tour, sadly came to an end in the autumn of 1974. A year later, the Phantom would be replaced at RAF Bruggen in the strike/attack and reconnaissance role by the SEPECAT Jaguar.

I resumed my association with the Phantom some five years later, having joined the Weapon Load Training Cell (WLTC) at RAF Leuchars. It was now my task to train Operational Turn Round (OTR) teams taken from the Station Engineering Wing, 43 and 111 Squadrons, though the Phantom's role was now that of air defence and so the weapons loaded were purely conventional AAMs and guns. Over a period of seven years I saw a great number of Phantom 'phixers' load and unload her battle station, before I bade a final farewell to the 'beast' in 1986.

Love it or loathe it, this aircraft always made a huge impression on all those associated with it. Me – I loved it!   F-4

Above: *RAF Akrotiri was high on our list of Phantom 'phixers' favourite places to hold an Armament Practice Camp (APC); 74 Squadron aircraft on their last F-4 APC.* AFM-DUNCAN CUBITT

Left: *Pete Shaw (middle, back row) and fellow armourers for 14 Squadron take a break from loading guns and missiles – or finding lost pencils in the cockpits.* AUTHOR

Above: *The Spanish Air Force Ala 12 unit based at Torrejón operates 14 RF-4C Phantoms.* LUIGINO CALIARO
Right: *RF-4Cs carry framing, panoramic and mapping cameras in three stations in the nose. Some have also been modified to carry a LOROP-camera (66 inch/168cm focal length) in camera stations two and three.*
Below: *The Boeing 707 tankers assigned to the co-located Esc 451 at Torrejón are used for strategic, long-distance missions. The Spanish RF-4Cs are equipped with both the probe/drogue and boom air to air refuelling systems.* ALA 123 VIA AUTHOR

D URING the 1970s and early 1980s, the Base Aérea de Torrejón, near Madrid, was not only the home of the USAF 16th Air Force, assigned to defend NATO's southern flank and a stepping-stone to the Middle East, but it also housed Europe's largest MDD F-4 Phantom force – 401st Tactical Fighter Wing/USAFE (612th/613th/614th Tactical Fighter System) and Ala de Casa (Air Wing) 12 of the Spanish EdA (Escuadrón 121/122).

Made up at one time of USAF D-models and EdA (Spanish Air Force) C-models, this 'bi-national/five squadron' Phantom force was gradually reduced in size. In April 1983, the 401st TFW (tailcode 'TJ'), which was de-activated in 1991 after the Spanish Government voted to evict US combat units from its territory, became the second USAFE wing to equip with General Dynamics F-16 Fighting Falcons. In April 1989, EdA's Ala12 started its transition to the multi-role MDD EF-18A/B Hornet fighters, bequeathing its Phantom heritage to the small-scale co-located 123 Escuadrón de Reconociemento Fotografico (Photographic Reconnaissance Squadron). Having gradually expanded, Esc 123 now has 14 RF-4C Phantoms and is fully responsible for

Spanish RF-4Cs

Stefan Degraef **looks at the Spanish RF-4C programme.**

all Tactical Reconnaissance (Reconociemento Tactico) of the EdA and the Spanish Armed Forces.

PEACE ALFA

Originating from a Hispano-US military co-operation agreement signed on March 26, 1953, the Spanish 'Phantom era' took off in June 1971 with the delivery of 36 ex-USAF F-4C Phantom II aircraft to Torrejón. These second-hand Phantoms, transferred to the EdA within the framework of the MDAP/Mutual Defence Aid Programme and code-named PEACE ALFA, had previously served with the 81st Tactical Fighter Wing (USAFE) at RAF Bentwaters, UK, becoming redundant after being replaced by more modern D-models. In order to replace the remaining obsolete F-86F Sabres and F-104G Starfighters, the Phantom all-weather interceptors were assigned to Ala 12 at Torrejón AB, equipping Esc 121 (Poker) and 122 (Tennis). To support the Phantom operations and provide a valuable air-refuelling capability, three ex-USAF KC-97L (TK.1 EdA-type designation) Stratotankers were purchased and used by the specially-activated Esc 123. Two additional C-97G Stratofreighters were

transferred from US ANG stocks to Albacete, Spain, and cannibalised for spare parts. Due to increasing maintenance problems and to the small 'speed window' between the Stratotanker's maximum speed and the Phantom's minimum, which put in jeopardy the safety of air-refuelling operations, these obsolete Boeings were withdrawn in August 1976. This was followed a year later by the premature disbanding of Esc 123. Although several programmes were brought in to replace the initial F-4C aircraft – designated C.12 ('c' for 'caza') in Spanish service – by more capable E-models, all these plans were put on ice. Instead it was agreed to transfer four additional ex-USAF C-models to Spain to make up for fleet attrition. At the same time that four additional C-models were transferred to Spain, four second-hand RF-4C-28-MC Phantom II reconnaissance aircraft were delivered to the EdA as part of Project PEACE ALFA II. These Phantoms (EdA CR.12 Caza Reconociemento) were taken from the operational inventory of the 363rd Tactical Reconnaissance Wing (Shaw AFB/SC) in order to boost and upgrade the Spanish AF reconnaissance assets, which comprised Northrop RF-5A Freedom Fighters

The purchase of a former US ANG-tripartite reconnaissance intelligence centre greatly enhanced the operational autonomy of the squadron, being able to deploy 'out-of-area' during (inter)national exercises.

(Spanish designation CR.9) and – to a lesser degree – Mirage IIIEEs, equipped with a single Omera 60 camera. Having previously been operated by both the Phantom fighter squadrons at Torrejón, an independent Escuadrilla de Reconociemento (Reconnaissance Flight) was gradually formed to centralise recce operations.

Phantom replacement

In the late 1970s, the EdA initiated its ambitious Futuro Avion de Combate y Ataque (FACA) programme to replace some of its older aircraft (especially the F-4Cs at Torrejón) with a new 'second generation' fighter aircraft, which in May 1983 led to the purchase of 72 MDD EF-18A/B Hornet fighters. Slowly, the operational life of the F-4C was drawing to a close. Shortly after the smooth introduction of the EF-18 Hornet, the EdA initiated a second and almost similar Sistema Avenzado de Reconociemento Aéreo (SARA) programme for the development and selection of an advanced night/all-weather reconnaissance system to replace its daylight-capable RF-5A Freedom Fighters and life-expired RF-4C Phantom IIs. Eventually the sophisticated ATARS reconnaissance pod was selected, which would be fitted on the EF-18 Hornet. The days of the 'recce Phantoms' seemed numbered.

As the development and introduction of this real-time recce pod would take longer than had been expected, the EdA had no choice but to look for an interim solution to retain its reconnaissance capabilities. Eight additional ex-USAF RF-4C Phantoms, all from the 165th TRS/123rd TRW Kentucky ANG, were purchased at a bargain price of US$ 20.3 million through the Foreign Military Sales (FMS) programme. On January 11 and 12, 1989, these 'new' Phantoms (EdA-serial CR.12-45/52) were flown by US ANG pilots in two groups from Louisville, Kentucky, to Torrejón after an eight-hour non-stop transit

flight and seven air-to-air refuellings.

Although these Phantoms were older than the original four (Block 23, 24, 25 and 26), their better all-round condition, flight potential and technical improvements – which included the installation of smokeless J79-GE-15E engines, improved radio hardware with ECCM-capabilities, VOR-ILS navigation systems, modern infra-red sensors and Itek AN/ARL-46 RWRs – were a welcome gift to the re-formed Esc 123. Five 'Kentucky' Phantoms were painted in the 'Hill One' camouflage scheme, and the other three finished in the green and grey 'European One'. Eventually all the EdA recce Phantoms received the overall grey Hornet-like colour scheme.

The arrival of these eight additional RF-4C Phantoms enabled the EdA to re-activate 123 Escuadrón de Reconociemento Fotografico at Torrejón AB. Initially, the squadron used

several former Esc 121/122 F-4C Phantom IIs for the conversion and operational training of its new pilots, coming from various fighter units of the EdA. During the conversion phase, the recce Phantoms were flown more than once by pilots of Esc 121/122 in anticipation of their Hornet conversion at Zaragoza AB. Until May 1990, Esc 123 also used these C-models as 'target-tugs' with a TDU-10 target-dart for air-to-air gunnery practice sessions and as test-beds for new armament and weapons systems for the benefit of Ala 54 at Torrejón. This unit, known since 1992 as CLAEX (Centro Logistico de Armemento y Experimentacion del EdA) is responsible for the development and operational testing of all the armament and weapons systems of the EdA. After completion of its Inspection and Repair as Necessary (IRAN) overhaul at CASA at Getafe-Madrid, one original RF-4C was delivered to Esc 123 but was withdrawn from service a few months later. Finally, on April 23, 1989, Esc 123 (Titan) regained its operational status at Torrejón. The last operational F-4C mission was flown on September 13, 1990. Afterwards all original RF/F-4Cs still owned by the USAF were put in external store at Torrejón, anticipating their final transfer to the Bardenas-Reales bombing range in northern Spain to be used as ground targets.

Phantom upgrade

Because of the operational withdrawal from the reconnaissance role of the RF-5A Freedom Fighters of Ala 21, based at Moron, the cancellation of the ATARS/F-18 programme in the USA, and the impossibility of financing and developing such a complex programme alone, the EdA decided on a multi-stage upgrade programme for its RF-4C Phantoms. During the first phase, all eight Phantoms were fitted with a fixed in-flight refuelling probe — developed by Israel Aircraft Industries (IAI) for the Israel Air Force. This allowed compatibility with the hose/drogue refuelling system used by the EdA Lockheed KC-130H (TK.10) Hercules and Boeing B707-331C (T.17) tankers. After this was installed, EdA-Phantoms (still with their original USAF refuelling systems) were able to receive fuel from all types of tankers, which greatly enhanced their operational capability

and flexibility. Initially qualified only for daylight refuelling operations, Esc 123 gained its night-time qualification in January 1996. Nowadays, at least two in-flight refuelling missions are flown every week by Esc 123 to allow its Phantom crews to retain their qualifications, these missions being to receive fuel from Hercules tankers during low-level low-speed tactical mission profiles. The Boeing 707 tankers assigned to the co-located Esc 451 are used for strategic, long-distance missions or for transatlantic ferry flights for Spain's EF-18 Hornet force.

Using a French-Hispanic bilateral air-refuelling interoperability programme, the CR-12 Phantom was certified in April 1997 to receive fuel from the Boeing C-135FR and Transall C-160NG Capricorne tankers of the French Armée de l'Air.

The second stage of the update programme was more radical. A five-month avionics update was initiated, based on operational experience gained by an EdA pilot during teaching practice with the 192nd RS/152nd RG Nevada ANG. The original Texas Instruments AN/APG-99 radar was replaced by the digital solid-state AN/APQ-172 terrain-following radar. A new Inertial Navigation System (INS), slaved to the Navigation and Weapons Delivery System (NWDS) was installed, together with a 1553B digital databus, enabling the smooth input of all flight and mission parameters in the Mission Planning II (MS-II) and NWDS before take-off. Finally, all aircraft received a digital radar altimeter and some internal modifications to enable the recording of radar and sensor images on a videotape for debriefing purposes. These modifications made the Spanish Phantoms identical to their US ANG counterparts, paving the way for the possible additional transfer of redundant US Phantoms to the EdA, which would make up for any fleet attrition and enable Esc 123 to fulfil its reconnaissance mission into the next century.

Nevada connection

This second purchase (US$10.3 million) of six additional ex-USAF RF-4C Phantom IIs eventually materialised in 1995, partly inspired by the USAF's decision to retire its last available tactical reconnaissance Phantoms,

Above: *Returning to Esc 123's flightline in April 1999, RF-4C Phantom '12-67' is the only aircraft, retaining its original US-colour scheme. Having lost its 'Nevada-connection' after the final US ANG-Phantom withdrawal, Esc 123 strengthened its links with Greek and Turkish RF-4E Phantom units.*
Below: *Seen in the 'Last chance area' in April 1999, RF-4C '12-63' is the only 123 Phantom, still to have a fixed refuelling probe installed by CASA/Getafe.*

then in service with the Reno-based 192nd 'High Rollers'/Nevada ANG, by October 1 that year. Initially scheduled to arrive in Spain on October 10, all aircraft were finally delivered on October 24 (four aircraft) and November 14 (two aircraft). During the final leg of their transit flight from MCAS Cherry Point (NC) to Torrejón, these RF-4C Phantoms – still wearing full 'High Roller' markings and flown by US ANG crews – were intercepted over the Hispano-Portuguese border and escorted by EdA Phantoms.

Although some of these 'new' Phantoms were older than the EdA-Phantoms, their avionics and tactical equipment included, as well as the various Spanish update modifications, the installation of AN/ALE-40 chaff/flare dispenser, Have-Quick UHF/VHF radios, AIM-9L Sidewinder capability and AN/ARL-46 Radar Earning Receivers (RWRs). These RWRs, fitted on the entire RF-4C fleet, were tested in the spring of 1996 during operational trials over

the USAFE Polygon Electronic Warfare range in Germany. In 1997, Esc 123 were retrofitted for the second time, with the fixed refuelling probe installed on the 'new' Phantoms (nuevos) and incorporating ALE-40 chaff/flare and AIM-9 Sidewinder capability on the 'old' RF-4s (viejos), to create a much-desired EdA-Phantom standardisation.

From the early 1990s, the operational life of Esc 123 has included participation in various national exercises. The squadron has also started to strengthen its ties with other NATO Phantom reconnaissance units, resulting in a squadron exchange with Aufklärungsgeschwader 51 'Immelmann' at Bremgarten, Germany, and a flight simulator session with Aufklärungsgeschwader 52 of Leck, Germany, flying RF-4E Phantoms. Eventually these annual simulator sessions, used to simulate emergency situations, were organised at Reno-Cannon IAP, home base of the 192nd RS/152nd RG Nevada ANG. An exchange pilot programme was also initiated with the 192nd RS, enabling one EdA crew to fly ANG Phantoms and one ANG crew – often qualified pilot instructors – to operate in Spain. Sadly, this exchange programme ended in 1996, a depressing result of the American decision to withdraw the RF-4C Phantoms from operational service. Unable to purchase the redundant Nevada simulator for financial reasons, Esc 123 moved its simulator training to Larissa, in Greece, using a former Luftwaffe RF-4E simulator transferred to the 110 Pteriga Mahis (Combat Wing) in 1993 following the withdrawal of the last Luftwaffe RF-4E Phantoms.

After the Nevada exchange programme, Esc123 – along with the EF-18 Hornet squadrons at Torrejón – quickly strengthened its ties with the Luftwaffe, which resulted in a new exchange pilot programme. Initially focused only on the EF-18 Hornet, Esc 123 received its first German exchange Weapons Systems Operator (WSO) in January 1998. After spending several months at Spain's military

Above: *Being assigned to Esc 123 in July 1998, Major Horst Kunzer (left), a former Luftwaffe RF-4E and Tornado WSO, is the first European Phantom exchange crew member, replacing several US ANG pilots and WSOs, on exchange postings in the early/mid-1990s.*
Left: *Having no dedicated twin-stick trainers, the forward view of the instructor-pilot – and WSO during standard flying operations – is obstructed by the aircraft's threat warning panel.*

With an average aircrew age of 28, some of the 1960s-built Phantoms are older than their 1970s-born aircrew.

academy learning Spanish, Major Horst Kunzer (36), a former Tornado WSO previously assigned to the Schleswig-Jagel based AG51, began his RF-4C conversion course in July 1998 at the beginning of a two-year posting to Torrejón. Familiar with Phantom recce operations, having flown almost 700 hours on Luftwaffe RF-4Es with 521 'Tiger' Squadron at Leck during the early 1990s, and up to date with the most modern recce tactics and techniques as a Tornado WSO, Kunzer is a welcome asset in the unit's quest for operational maturity, especially after its recent boom in aircraft availability.

Search for maturity

As it became a full-sized operational reconnaissance unit, enabling the EdA to elaborate joint recce/strike operations, Esc 123 took part in various national and multi-national air exercises.

During January 1995, it participated for the first time in a large-scale 'out-of-area' NATO exercise in Norway, STRONG RESOLVE, based temporarily at Rygge AB, near Oslo, where it operated in unfamiliar and wintry conditions. Initially hampered by the lack of air-deployable containers to convey photo-processing, interpreting, developing and data-transferring equipment, in November 1996 it was able to purchase a redundant former US ANG tripartite Reconnaissance Intelligence Centre (RIC). Having gained this degree of mobility, Esc 123 deployed in March 1997 to Son San Juan (Palma de Mallorca/Baleares) to take part in the national DAPEX exercise. Using the RIC for the first time during the exercise, pictures were transferred to EdA-MACOM's (Mando Aero de Combate) HQ in Madrid. Spain's strategic location and that of its dependent islands, the Canaries and the Balearics, lends increasing importance to maritime operations, as testified to by its multiple long-range maritime reconnaissance training missions. In order to increase their operational experience, Esc 123 aircrew often visit other NATO reconnaissance squadrons. On these occasions, at least one operational training mission is carried out using the host's recce facilities. In September 1996, Esc 123 visited the Turkish Air Force's 1nci AJÜ (1st Air Wing) at Eskisehir for its annual ten-day squadron exchange, trading places with

six Turkish RF-4E Phantoms. In November 1996, the squadron exchange between the EF-18 Hornet-equipped Esc 121 and Jagdgeschwader 73, flying MiG-29 *Fulcrums* and F-4F Phantoms, was used to organise Dissimilar Air Combat Training (DACT) with the Russian-built MiG-29 *Fulcrums*. Additional Mixed Fighter Force Operations (MFFO) experience was gained during NATO's AMPLE TRAIN 97/1 maintenance exercise, organised at Torrejón in May 1997. It enabled Esc 123 to perform pre-strike reconnaissance and battle damage assessment missions in support of multi-national 'strike-packages' (USAFE F-15Es, RAF Tornados and Harriers, and a variety of participating F-16A/Cs). The squadron's real operational evaluation was AIRCENT's annual large-scale NATO Air Meet (NAM) 1998, organised at Zaragoza, Spain, and attended by almost 100 NATO front-line fighters and ground-attack aircraft. As the only reconnaissance squadron at NAM 1998, Esc 123's two RF-4C Phantoms were responsible for all 'pre-strike recce' during the various Combined Air Operations (COMAO), including a Tactical Air Support for Maritime Operations (TASMO) mission against Spain's Armada *Principe de Asturias* carrier battle group, sailing in the Mediterranean.

Phantom Training

In spite of its rather small size, the entire pilot and WSO (OA/Operador de Armas) training and conversion syllabus is organised by Esc 123. Having successfully completed the Spanish EdA

advanced jet training course at Talavera la Real, each 'would-be' Phantom pilot starts his conversion with a month-long academic course. Afterwards all trainees initiate a first flying phase, comprising ten missions (general flying, IFR and formation flying) and a first check flight. During the second tactical conversion phase comprising 34 missions (visual low-levels, night-IFR, air/air refuelling and defensive Basic Fighter Manoeuvres (BFM), the future pilot or WSO learns to operate the Phantom as a tactical reconnaissance asset. Afterwards crews are awarded the CR1 (Combat Ready 1) status and included in daily flying operations, accumulating additional flying and tactical experience.

Challenged by a boom in aircraft availability – and operational workload – after receiving its final ex-US ANG Phantoms in 1995, and with no more former F-4C WSOs available for immediate integration, Esc 123 was forced to enlist and train at short notice a new generation of young 'factory-fresh' pilots and – more importantly – WSOs. After passing a preliminary in-depth medical selection, the new WSOs were given a 50-hour aeronautical instruction and awareness course on the ENEAR T-35 Tamiz at the Air Force's Academia General del Aire at Murcia-San Javier, followed by a similar, but shorter, course on the CASA C101 Aviojet jet-trainer.

Once at Torrejón, a five- to six-month long course, identical to the pilot syllabus and including academics and flying training, was taught to the new WSOs. Assigned to Esc 123's Primera (First) or Secunda (Second) Escuadrilla (Flights), the young and inexperienced WSOs, mostly second lieutenants in their mid-twenties, needed on average six months 'on the job' training to become operational and to join Esc 123's 16 member aircrew as operational WSOs.

Today, made up of a sound mix of experienced and ambitious young pilots and WSOs – some of them younger than their aircraft – Esc 123 is almost reaching operational maturity. However, due to the age of its 1960s recce 'Charlie Phantoms' and to the recent evolution in aerial warfare (stand-off, unmanned and high-tech strategic and tactical reconnaissance and information gathering hardware and vehicles, especially UAVs), the operational future of the Spanish CR-12 Phantom has been thrown into doubt. Its possible participation in multi-national NATO/UN peacekeeping operations has become increasingly uncertain, and its eventual replacement by a recce pod-carrying EF-18 version or a UAV is almost inevitable. **F-4**

Esc 123's flightline at Torrejón with six RF-4C Phantoms standing ready and waiting for their pilots and WSOs to start the day's flying programme. ALL PHOTOS, AUTHOR UNLESS STATED

Phantom Testers

Alan Christian Alpers looks at how US Navy Phantoms acquire another lease of life after retirement – testing new weaponry at Point Mugu.

ONCE THE big workhorses of the Vietnam War, they have now been retired to the desert of the southwestern United States. They sit there out of service, but by no means forgotten. Contrary to what one might think, once an aircraft is retired from a service inventory, it doesn't mean it ceases to have a useful life. This is the case with the F-4 'Phantom II' aircraft and its role with the Navy's test and evaluation laboratories. This aircraft, still being refurbished by the US Navy, contributes a vital role in the development of new weaponry and targeting at the Naval Air Warfare Center Weapons Division, located in Southern California.

Ranges

The Naval Air Warfare Center Weapons Division (NAWCWPNS) is the premier research, development, test and evaluation facility for conventional missile systems, weapons avionics, and associated sub-systems for the US Navy. Its two main sites, under one command, are located at the naval air stations at Point Mugu and China Lake, both in Southern California. Both bases survived the 1990s rounds of base closure by at least one count, due to their respective test ranges,

associated instrumentation, and co-located laboratory facilities. These two sites represent the last Navy bases still to utilise the Phantom II aircraft.

China Lake represents 38% of the Navy's real estate holdings, a land test range consisting of over a million acres. It also controls 17,000 sq miles (44,000km²) of overlying air space from ground to infinity. So seclusion, security, long-range test space, and 50 years of facility development make China Lake a highly-valued

laboratory asset. Land testing provides some benefits, the main ones being optical coverage and three-dimensional analysis, since trackers and cameras can be precisely fixed. Also, recovery of the test article is relatively easier than in open ocean. The British Ministry of Defence found this particular feature at China Lake to be highly desirable for trials of the ALARM missile, and built permanent facilities on the range during the 1990s. The Joint Trials Unit 32 conducted the tests.

Above: *NAWC-WD QF-4N 152983 is seen over a sea test range with an AQM-37C drone beneath the port wing.* US NAVY

Right: *NOLO QF-4F of the NAWC-AD lands at San Nicolas Island following a sortie over the sea range.* US NAVY

Carolina, is the refurbishing and droning facility for the Navy's F-4 aircraft. Once converted, the drone has the nomenclature of QF-4N or S.

The conversion basically restores the aircraft to flight qualifications, adds a camera in the nose to assist take-offs, landings and provide general video viewing; adds a radio control function to enable pilotless flight; and adds a small explosive package to dislodge the aircraft's wings (a safety feature in the event of a communication problem with the aircraft). The nose radar is removed to fit the command and control equipment in the aircraft. The Navy converted over 100 QF-4Ns, beginning in the early 1980s, with most serving on the West Coast test ranges. Now the Navy is exclusively converting F-4S aircraft for drone use, the 'N' version's supply having been depleted over years of testing. In the late 1990s, a global positioning (GPS) system became an added feature on the 'S' versions.

Once this aircraft is converted, it is flown from the East Coast to the West Coast for use at the Navy's ranges at NAWCWPNS. It is operated by the Weapons Test Squadron, located at Point Mugu. This squadron, the newest in the downsizing Navy, was established in October 1994 to provide aviation support to test programmes at the NAWCWPNS ranges. QF-4 maintenance is carried out by a contractor, a recent decision prompted by a commercial activities study.

At Point Mugu, a typical operation of a QF-4 may or may not involve a pilot during a range test. If a pilot's safety is an issue, the aircraft is flown, piloted, to San Nicolas Island. While these aircraft are capable of flying No Onboard Live Operator (NOLO) operations, the Navy does not fly pilotless from the air station at Point Mugu for safety reasons. The station is surrounded by cities, and approaches to the airfield often involve flight paths over nearby centres of population. Because of this, for a particular test a pilot may fly to San Nicolas Island and, once there, may exit. The aircraft is then flown NOLO from the Range Operations Center at Point Mugu for the prospective test. Thus, it is a direct line of sight, with the Laguna Peak attributes making this possible. China Lake, where the airfield is amid the test ranges, flies NOLO from the runway through the planned test.

Controlling the flight in a NOLO state is done from the Range Operations Center at Point Mugu and the Range Control Center at China Lake. Generally, retired military aviators with F-4 flying experience are contracted to fly the aircraft remotely. Two systems are available. One, a simulated cockpit with a stick, controls, and instruments gives the "feel' of flying the aircraft. The view provided by a nose-mounted camera is projected in front of the pilot back at the range centres. Once airborne, with nothing but blue sky as a reference, the pilot then flies by instruments over a predetermined path. The second method of flight control is digital. Sitting in a chair, the pilot basically controls the flight the same way, though the sensation of flying is much less realistic. There are several consoles in each range centre: at Point Mugu

Conversely, Point Mugu offers a different range asset, the Sea Test Range. The Naval Air Station Point Mugu is located on the California coast about 60 miles (96.5km) north of Los Angeles. From here, NAWCWPNS controls 36,000 sq miles (93,200km²) of instrumented test range in the Pacific Ocean, and operates an outlying landing facility on San Nicolas Island, 60 miles (96.5km) west of Los Angeles. This island belongs to the Navy and, most importantly, is outside most commercial shipping lanes, allowing for easy security, seclusion and safety.

The key geological feature is the 1,457ft (444m) high Laguna Peak, located on the mainland just south of Point Mugu. It offers a line of sight to San Nicolas, thus providing real-time data links, microwave transmissions, and look-down radar to observe commercial shipping movements. This is imperative to the operation of drones on the island via commands provided from the mainland's Point

Mugu Range Operations Center.

NOLO

With these ranges, NAWCWPNS depends largely on its use of targets in engagement scenarios to test new weapons, software, or targeting technologies. It also serves as a large range for foreign customers, testing various weapons and avionics. In these tests, targets are of primary importance. Targets can be anything from a relatively simple towed item, a more complex simulated missile, or a fully-restored, operational Phantom aircraft converted to a target – the ultimate radio-controlled aircraft.

The F-4N, featured here, served many additional flight hours as a drone for the US Navy. Usually mothballed in the Arizona desert at Davis Monthan AFB, Arizona (preferred for its low-moisture environment) the aircraft are shipped to Cherry Point to be reborn. The Naval Air Station at Cherry Point, North

A Naval Weapons Test Squadron Point Mugu QF-4N receives fuel from a Kansas ANG KC-135E over San Nicolas Island during a Tomahawk cruise missile operation. US NAVY

they boast the ability to put as many as five NOLO targets in the air for one test.

Different roles

The QF-4N served many different roles at NAWCWPNS. Piloted or pilotless, the aircraft provided some important real world, simulated targets for the development of new weapons systems, avionics for developing aircraft, and target acquisition tests. Roles included serving as a launch platform, a tow platform, flying a missile trajectory, flare and chaff dispensing, serving as the primary aggressor aircraft target in a missile test, and even flying chase for cruise missile tests fired from the Pacific Ocean to land base sites at China Lake (180 miles [290km] inland) or beyond.

The drones are capable of carrying a variety of targets and missile simulants. In a missile-against-missile test, or in a ship defence test, the NOLO capability is important since no pilot is in the air when the missiles or simulants are tested. One target may be an AQM-37, which is capable of simulating a supersonic, incoming missile. A drone may also carry fielded weapons for launch, such as sidewinders or Zuni rockets. No matter what the test, unanticipated problems make the NOLO aspect of the QF-4 a desirable safety feature.

In a targeting role, the aircraft itself may simulate an inbound missile, either against a ship at sea, or against a fixed land target at either Point Mugu or China Lake. The plane's ability to fly the same trajectory many times cuts test costs and assures repeatability. Usually targeting will have a pilot on board. The targeting tests may take place in order to work out software problems, test new target acquisition technologies, test sensors or test tracking with either lasers or video theodolites.

Another test may see the same drone towing a target. If a missile is to be used in a targeting test, it is cheaper to 'kill' a simple towed item than to destroy a fully restored QF-4. The cost of restoring a Phantom II and the conversion is relatively expensive. If destruction is unnecessary, the testing philosophy is to save the aircraft and kill the cheaper towed item.

The Navy's QF-4s provide the ability to handle high-g banking manoeuvres, making them ideally suited for both flare dispensing and other countermeasure tests. New targeting systems can be tested against the drones while the drones defend themselves, replicating a typical engagement scenario. New types of flares or acquired threat systems may be used.

Sometimes it is necessary to test a weapons system in a real-world environment against an aggressor aircraft. In such cases, a newly upgraded surface-to-air or air-to-air missile may need to pass development or operational testing for final deployment to the Fleet. In such cases a fully restored drone, flying NOLO, will have to be sacrificed. Again, the controlled land or ocean environment allows for the destroyed target to impact the surface – ocean or land – with assured safety. Between six and 12 drones may meet this fate each year, depending on range customers and their requirements.

Finally, a non-target role played by QF-4s is that of chase aircraft during tests on the Tomahawk cruise missile. During these test operations, a pilot flies in the aircraft. A typical test would see the launch of a cruise missile from a submarine located in the Sea Test Range (from, for instance, a location like San Clemente Island, the southernmost coastal island in the west), and the flight of the weapon north over the ocean to unpopulated areas around Santa Barbara and inland to impact areas at China Lake, over 200 miles (320km) away. A special 'corridor' is available for defence test flights of the cruise missile, and in fact, the missile could fly to impact areas in the state of Utah, over 1,000 miles (1,600km) away.

These drone aircraft, with their nose cameras and wing-mounted camera pods, can easily transmit video images during the flight of the cruise missile, in real-time back to the station at Point Mugu and, furthermore, to programme sponsors or Pentagon officials in Washington DC on the east coast. With live operators on board, spotting is easy and conditions during flight can be easily verified. Typically, the Tomahawk missile's range prohibits full flight coverage, so another QF-4 will join the chase and take over the role during the flight.

As an aside, the F-4 contributes further as a test platform at Point Mugu. The Weapons Test Squadron operates a YF-4J aircraft for ejection seat testing. Originally at China Lake, this aircraft is known as the Naval Aircraft Common Ejection System (NACES) test aircraft, and is capable of flying remotely and firing ejection seats to test successful emergency egress for aviators. It is currently testing seats and new parachute designs both for the Royal Canadian Air Force and the National Aviation and Space Agency, NASA. So while the Phantom II aircraft has been phased out of the Navy's forces, it still serves an active role in the Navy's labs in Southern California. The unique sound of the F-4 aircraft is still heard in nearby communities, and aviation enthusiasts are still surprised when they spot the retired Phantoms flying about. The QF-4N served for many years as the best real world target for the US Navy. Whether a QF-4N or QF-4S, the Phantom II aircraft has provided a high-performance test vehicle to assure the best weapons for the Fleet. Its role, once thought to be over, has flourished, and its contribution as a 'senior citizen' in the aviation community continues to this day. F-4

author's note

Special thanks for assistance to Steve Boster and Vance Vasquez, public affairs officials at China Lake and Point Mugu, respectively. Additionally, the Phantom II Society holds conventions each year at various bases still flying the aircraft. Its e-mail address is http://users.aol.com/f14ro/private/f4homepage.html for more information.
Alan Christian Alpers is a freelance writer and former Public Affairs Officer at China Lake and Point Mugu.

QF-4J 151473 of the NWTS is involved in ejector seat trials. It is known as the Naval Aircraft Common Ejection System (NACES) test aircraft. CHRISTOPH KUGLER

Hellenic guardians

Above: *A three-ship formation of 338 MPK F-4Es – all acquired from US ANG stocks in 1991. These aircraft now operate with 337 MPK at Larisa.*
Right: *Most of the Greek pilots flying the Phantom II are highly experienced. Indeed, back-seaters must amass 300 hours before they can transfer to the front seat!*

Above: *Parked on the ramp at Andravida is F-4E 68-0424 of the 338 MPK, which operated with the 113th TFS/Indiana ANG at Terre Haute until its transfer on August 1, 1991.* AFM-ALAN WARNES
Below: *An F-4E of 339MPK taxies out for another sortie at Andravida. This South East Asia colour scheme has now been replaced with the new 'Ghost' scheme.*
AFM-ALAN WARNES

Above: *The new Ghost camouflage scheme is inspired by the F-16 and blends in very effectively with the blue skies and waters of the Aegean. The aircraft seen here belongs to 338 MPK at Andravida.*
Right: *The interior of an RF-4E front cockpit.*

Above: *Of the 27 ex-GAF RF-4Es delivered to the Hellenic Air Force, approximately ten never made it to frontline service. This aircraft was one of two being used as a spares source at Andravida in July 1995.* AFM-ALAN WARNES
Below: *This F-4E, seen taxying at Larisa, is loaded with a Dart aerial target, used to train pilots in the use of the Vulcan cannon.* ALL PHOTOS, KOSTAS DIMITROPOULOS UNLESS STATED

Aegean Upgrades

⊙ **GREECE**

Georg Mader reports on PEACE ICARUS the Greek F-4E upgrade

AFTER YEARS of negotiations, in August 1997 the Greek Cabinet's defence committee selected Daimler-Benz to upgrade the F-4 Phantom for the Hellenic Air Force (HAF - Elliniki Polimiki Aeroporia). Greece started to receive its 92 brand new F-4Es in 1974. They were joined in 1991 by 28 ex-ANG F-4Es, that today operate with the 337 MPK (Mira Pantos Kerou - all weather Fighter Squadron) at Larissa. This is one of three F-4E squadrons within the HAF, the other two being the 338th and 339th MPK at Andravida. To prolong F-4 operations until 2015, all the remaining 109 airframes are to undergo a Structural Life Extension Programme – 38 will be modified by DASA, while Hellenic Aerospace Industries (HAI) will apply its own structural life extension programme to the other 70 airframes.

The programme, PEACE ICARUS 2000, is worth around $317 million and was awarded after fierce competition. DASA's Military Aircraft Division was chosen after it clinched a renewed round of bidding with Boeing (Rockwell), which had full support within US political and commercial circles. Controversially, Israel Aircraft Industries had offered a 'Phantom 2000' package to Greece, only to withdraw the offer when it looked like it might endanger its prospects of modernising the Turkish Air Force F-4s. After a first round of bids were rejected, PEACE ICARUS 2000 was developed by DASA in close co-operation with its Greek industrial partner HAI, Hughes Radar Systems and Elbit Systems of Israel. DASA allegedly cut its bid price by one third after the first round, and it is understood that former German Defence Minister Volker Rühe personally intervened – however, this was never confirmed.

PEACE ICARUS is based on the experience DASA gained from the successful conclusion of the KWS (Kampfwertsteigerung or Improved Combat Efficiency – see *German Evolution*, page 56) modernisation programme which upgraded 110 German Air Force F-4Fs in 1997. It will dramatically improve the mission effectiveness, sensor capabilities and weapon delivery for aspects of air-to-air and air-to-ground combat.

The first HAF aircraft to undergo the work (serial no 01523, named *Princess of Andravida*) arrived in Manching during autumn 1997. After completing the first two Phantoms here, the rest will be dealt with by HAI at Tanagra, near Athens.

There are few visible changes to the aircraft, as the work has involved modifications to the J-79 engines, structural overhauls to extend the service life for another 6,000 hours and

Above: *The AGM-130 (middle) will substantially boost the HAF's attack capability.*
AFM-ALAN WARNES

Below: *The second Hellenic Air Force F-4E under a mass of wires and cable is tested in the DASA maintenance hangar.* AUTHOR

fitting four Frazer-Nash ejector launchers for belly-mounted AMRAAMs. DASA will integrate the new avionics and sub-systems, as it did for the German Luftwaffe Phantoms.

The basic package consists of a new laser inertial gyro embedded GPS/INU programme with Global Positioning System, a GEC CPU-143/A digital air data computer and a new 1553B databus, connected to a new fire-control Elbit Systems computer. In the cockpit, the entire layout is state-of-the-art Hands-On Throttle and Stick technology, which includes multi-function colour displays, a head-up display/up-front control panel unit, with an equivalent in the rear, and an improved Identification Friend or Foe system. The radar warning receiver is now a Litton ALR-68(V)-2. A key element of the programme is the Hughes AN/APG-65GY radar, with a slightly enhanced power output and improved modulation correlation, user interface and lower maintenance time compared to the standard - 65 radar.

The new F-4E version for the HAF can now deliver a broad variety of intelligent long-range air-to-air and air-to-ground weapons. Beside the AIM-120 AMRAAM, it is now possible to use the GBU-16 or the AGM-130 guided air-to-ground stores. Provision is also included for future use of the IRIS-T.

Completion of the first airframe on April 28, 1999, marked the beginning of the flight test phase, when the prototype took off from DASA's Manching flight test centre. The crew comprised Luftwaffe test pilot Robert Hierl and DASA navigator Richard Gütter. During their 45-minute sortie, they not only expanded the aircraft's flight envelope to Mach 1.5 and an altitude of 45,000ft (13,700m), but also marked the beginning of another chapter in the long history of the famous Phantom.

When *Princess of Andravida* leaves Manching, after approximately 25 test flights, HAI will upgrade 36 further HAF Phantoms in Greece with support from DASA. DASA claims the Hellenic Air Force will then operate the most effective and powerful F-4 version of the 1,000+ Phantom aircraft in service throughout the world. Company officials hope that the successful completion of the Greek modernisation programme will enable DASA to compete more effectively for combat aircraft upgrade contracts in the well-established international market.

Princess of Andravida is the prototype PEACE ICARUS *aircraft. It made its first flight on April 28, 1999, and is currently embarking on a 25-sortie test programme.* AUTHOR

TURKEY

Serhat Guvenc looks at the Turkish Phantom upgrade programme

The first two upgraded F-4E Phantom 'Terminators' as they are currently referred to, taxi out of the IAI Lahav facility at Ben Gurion Airport. Both aircraft, serials 68-0498 and 73-1032, left for Eskisehir on January 24. IAI

THE TURKISH Air Force's F-4E Phantom modernisation requirement became urgent towards the end of the 1970s. In the early 1980s, this developed into two separate programmes; aircraft modernisation and modernisation of the electronic warfare (EW) system, in particular the ALQ-119 jammer pods, the ALR-46 RWR and the ALE-40 chaff/flare dispensers. In the 1990s, the F-4 modernisation plan gained momentum and was seen as a whole project; both airframe and electronics. Turkey selected IAI (Israeli Aircraft Industries Ltd)-Lahav division to upgrade its 54 F-4Es to Phantom 2000 standards, a deal worth US $632 million. The first modernised prototype made its official flight on March 1, 1999, at the IAI facilities at Ben Gurion Airport, Tel Aviv, although it had made a first test flight on February 11 that year.

The first two aircraft, 73-1025 and 73-1032, were delivered to IAI in February 1997 and were later joined by a third aircraft 68-0498. Testing was carried out by a joint team of IAI and TuAF pilots. Phantom 73-1025 is the pre-production aircraft and will eventually be returned to Turkey. Delivery of the first two aircraft to the Turkish Air Force's 111 Filo took place officially on January 27, although they had arrived from IAI Lahav some four days earlier.

Pilot training was undertaken in Israel, the other unit to receive the 'Terminator' will be 171 Filo at Erhac.

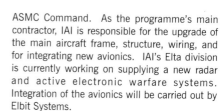

The Israeli upgrade includes an IAI Elta EL/M2032 multi mode fire control radar (seen here in a MiG 21). AFM-ALAN WARNES

Ten more aircraft are currently undergoing serial production modernisation and will be delivered at a rate of one per month.

Implementation of the F-4 upgrade is divided between IAI and the Turkish AF aircraft maintenance facility, the 1 Aviation Supply and Maintenance Centre (ASMC) Command at Eskisehir. Twenty-six aircraft will be upgraded by IAI and 28 by 1

ASMC Command. As the programme's main contractor, IAI is responsible for the upgrade of the main aircraft frame, structure, wiring, and for integrating new avionics. IAI's Elta division is currently working on supplying a new radar and active electronic warfare systems. Integration of the avionics will be carried out by Elbit Systems.

The upgrade is similar to that carried out on Israel Air Force aircraft, with the Turkish examples being given an avionics upgrade which includes complete re-wiring of the aircraft to incorporate a MIL STD 1553 multiplex databus. A new IAI/Elta EL/M-2032 fire control radar is also included. Other minor changes are multi-function displays, new head-up display (HUD), global positioning system/inertial navigation system (GPS/INS), a stores management system and an internal EW suite. These modifications will keep the Phantoms in service for 15 to 20 years.

Even at the start of negotiations between Turkey and Israel, Popeye I missiles had been part of the F-4 Phantom upgrade programme. Following initial talks in October 1998, a US $80 million contract covering 64 Popeye I missiles was signed between Turkey's Ministry of National Defence and Rafael of Israel. These missiles will equip the upgraded Turkish Phantoms.

Above: *111 'Panther' Filo officially took delivery of the first two aircraft on January 27. Pilots from the unit line up in front of the aircraft during the ceremony, note the weapons which include a laser guided bomb (centre). The bullets are arranged as 1 US, denoting 1st Main Jet Base.* TuAF
Inset: *The F-4E Terminator badge.* TuAF

TurkishTooms

Turkey acquired its first batch of F-4s in 1974 and, as Serhat Guvenc recounts, has continued to acquire, upgrade and operate the aircraft.

IN THE 1970s the Turkish Air Force (TuAF) was using F-100C/D Super Sabres in the fighter/bomber role and there was an urgent need for a powerful modern next-generation fighter/bomber aircraft. Turkey ordered 40 F-4Es from McDonnell Douglas, financing the purchase from its national budget and not an American Military Assistance Programme (MAP). The 40 Phantoms were delivered under the PEACE DIAMOND 1 programme, and the TuAF also received weapons such as laser and optically guided bombs, AGM-65 Maverick missiles, AIM-9 Sidewinder and AIM-7 Sparrow missiles, and ALQ-119 ECM pods.

Cyprus

Prior to the delivery of the first batch, Turkish pilots trained on USAF F-4Ds in May 1974 at McDill AFB. While pilot training and the manufacture of Turkish Phantoms were taking place, the Turkish Armed Forces (TAF) landed in Northern Cyprus on July 22, 1974. The first two Turkish F-4E Phantoms (tail numbers 73-1016 and 73-1017), arrived at 1 AJU (Ana

Above: *Turkey acquired 46 RF-4Es from Germany as part of Project KAAN, of which 12 were used as spares and ended up with the 1st Aviation Supply and Repair Centre at Eskisehir. The remainder were split between 113 and 173 Filos at Eskisehir and Erhac respectively. Here, 69-7458/'1-7458' of 113 Filo performs an overshoot at its home base.* AFM-ALAN WARNES

Top: *An F-4E of 111 'Panther' Filo squadron taxies out at Eskisehir.* AFM-ALAN WARNES

Jet Ussu/main jet base) in Eskisehir on August 30, 1974. The first batch of F-4Es, consisting of 22 aircraft, was flown to Turkey by American ferry pilots. No.1 AJU Eskisehir became known as 'The Home of Phantoms' and the first F-4E squadron, 113 Filo was activated. Pilot training was undertaken by the first Turkish Phantom pilots who had trained in the USA. The rest of the 18 F-4Es arrived in 1978 – some sources believe that the late delivery of this last batch was due to a US embargo which had been imposed because the Turkish Armed Forces had landed in Northern Cyprus.

The first 40 brand-new aircraft came direct

from St Louis, Missouri. Turkey ordered a further 40 aircraft – under the PEACE DIAMOND programme – from McDonnell Douglas (32 F-4Es and 8 RF-4Es) in 1977, paying for these too from its national budget. The 5,000th Phantom built by the St Louis plant was delivered to the TuAF with this second order – a special ceremony taking place in Missouri on May 20, 1978. The date also marked the 20th anniversary of the first Phantom Flight. This aircraft was specially painted for the ceremony (see contents pages), though the TuAF later re-painted it in a standard Vietnam-era camouflage scheme. The 5,000th Phantom (77-0290) was flown for many years and despite two major accidents, it still flies with 111 Filo at 1 AJU Eskisehir.

After the CYPRUS PEACE Operation in 1974, F-4E Phantoms replaced the F-100 Super Sabres, and eventually all the former F-100 squadrons converted to the F-4E Phantom. The conversion continued as the first RF-4Es entered service, replacing the venerable RF-84Fs in the TuAF inventory. After delivery of the first 72 F-4Es and eight RF-4E Phantoms, 15 ex-USAF Phantoms came from

A 'Hill Gray' F-4E of 112 Filo hits the runway at Eskisehir. AFM-ALAN WARNES

AMARC Davis Monthan AFB in 1981 under the Military Assistance Programme. Attrition levels were high and by 1983, 15 aircraft had been written off. Consequently, another 15 ex-USAF Phantoms arrived from Davis Monthan the following year. The third delivery took place in 1986, with the arrival of 15 ex-USAF Phantoms from the same source, with another 40 ex-USAF Phantoms arriving the following year. After the first 72 F-4Es purchased by Turkey, 85 more came direct from the USAF. The TuAF organised seven operational F-4E squadrons, with 15 aircraft in each, and by 1990, the inventory included 157 F-4Es, plus eight RF-4Es, bringing the total to 165 aircraft.

Desert Storm support

Aircraft continued to be lost over the subsequent years, and in 1989 132 Filo was temporarily disbanded due to a lack of aircraft. In 1991-92, after Operation DESERT STORM, the US sent 40 ex-USAF F-4Es to Turkey as thanks for its help and support during the campaign. Announcement of the delivery was made after a weekend of talks at Camp David in late March 1991 between US President George Bush and President Turgut zal. An initial delivery of four F-4Es took place at Eskisehir on March 25, though bad weather forced one F-4E to divert to another TuAF base. These 40 F-4Es were the last Phantoms the TuAF received from the USAF, bringing the total to 205 (197 F-4Es + 8 RF-4Es), and marking the end of the ex-USAF Phantom transfers.

The US deliveries were followed by German Phantoms (RF-4Es) in 1992. The German Government had earmarked 46 RF-4E Phantoms for Turkey as a result of the German/USSR accord which came into place after re-unification. The Luftwaffe had completed life extension work on its fleet, bringing the total life cycle to 6,000 flight hours. When they were delivered to the TuAF, the Luftwaffe RF-4Es had at least 2,500 flight hours remaining.

In December 1992, the first 12 RF-4Es were delivered to Turkey to be cannibalised for spares. The remaining 34 were designated for basic life extension by MBB and radar upgrades by TST (now both DASA) – this being financed through Turkey's national budget. TST upgraded the RF-4E's Texas Instruments APQ-99 radar to APQ-172. However, under intense pressure from opposition groups, the German Government temporarily brought a halt to arms transfers in order to investigate accusations that former German equipment had been misused in Turkey. This directly affected the deliveries of those RF-4Es taken out of Luftwaffe service. After the ban was lifted and parliamentary approval granted, the first upgraded RF-4E was handed over to the TuAF on April 21, 1993. Delivery of the remaining aircraft was completed in 1995.

A total of 46 ex-GAF RF-4E aircraft has been delivered under the KAAN project (34 going to 113 and 173 Recce Squadrons) and 12 have been used as spares. The TuAF's main overhaul facility, 1 Air Supply and Repair Centre (ASRC) in Eskisehir, worked extensively on ex-GAF RF-4Es in order to standardise the recce fleet, which comprises eight US RF-4Es and 34 Luftwaffe RF-4Es. As part of this work, integration of electronic warfare suites and wiring for carrying weapons was introduced on

all the Turkish RF-4Es. The TuAF has received a total of 251 Phantoms (F-4E/RF-4E or spares), and 50 or 60 of them have been written off in accidents. At the moment, the Air Force operates between 150 and 180 Phantoms spread over eight squadrons (20 aircraft in each) – which is reckoned to be the largest F-4 Phantom fleet in the world. After the F-16 Fighting Falcon, the F-4E Phantom still forms the backbone of the TuAF's fighter/bomber force.

No.1 Aviation Supply and Maintenance Centre, Eskisehir, is the main overhaul facility for F-4E Phantoms and General Electric J-79-17A engines, and has overhauled more than 350 Phantoms since 1979.

TuAF's F-4Es came from the following USAF units: 37th TFW George AFB, California; 337th TFS Seymour Johnson AFB, North Carolina; 110th TFS Air National Guard; 141st TFS ANG New Jersey, and AMARC Davis Monthan AFB. Naturally, the camouflage schemes were different – Vietnam (three-tone South East camouflage), Euro-1 (two-tone grey) and Lizard (three-tone green). Phantoms camouflaged in Euro-1 were sent direct to air defence squadrons. Some Air National Guard Phantoms arrived with 'Shark's Mouth' and 'Tiger's Head' artwork on the noses – the 'Shark's Mouth' examples being reserved by the air defence squadrons. Interestingly, there were some 'MiG Killer' Phantoms among one of the deliveries: 338 and 301 'MiG Killer' Phantoms are still flying with the TuAF at Eskisehir. They also carried a red star on their air intakes when they were delivered. Turkish Phantoms continued in their original delivery colours until their overhaul time came. Currently, TuAF Phantoms have two different camouflage schemes applied during overhaul.

Aircraft from air defence units are painted in Euro-1, with aircraft from bomber units painted in Vietnam-style camouflage. An important change was introduced to the TuAF F-4E fleet in 1998, with aircraft losing their large white-on-black numbers on the fuselage (denoting the base and the last digits of the tail number). They now only carry their tail number.

Some of the ex-USAF F-4Es aircraft came equipped with the AVQ-23A Pave Spike pod. In addition, 72 TuAF F-4Es carried Target Identification System Electro-Optical (TISEO) mounted on the left wing, though these were later removed. The ALQ-119 pod was the basic ECM pod carried.

Today, the home of the Turkish Phantoms is the 3.Ana Jet Us Komutanlg (3 Main Jet Base Command) located in Konya. No.131 Filo is the only TuAF squadron concerned with basic and combat readiness training for F-4E Phantom pilots and weapon systems operators (WSOs). After graduating from 2nci Ana Jet Us Komutanlg in Cigli-Izmir (basic and advanced jet training base), those selected as Phantom drivers go to Konya.

A new F-4E pilot receives 60 hours of academic training and 52 hours of combat flight training over a six-month period. Training also covers 15 hours in F-4E simulation before the flight sorties. No.131 Filo runs two different training programmes depending upon the type of mission the pilot will undertake – air defence or bombing. At the end of combat flight training, pilots undertake a standardisation flight with 132 Filo (Weapons and Tactics Squadron) which uses a mixture of F-4E and NF-5A aircraft. They are then transferred to an F-4E Phantom squadron at Eskisehir or Malatya. For upgrade details see *Aegean Upgrades* on page 38.

Above: *3.AJU at Konya is home to two squadrons (Filos). No.131 Filo is responsible for training Phantom pilots and WSOs, while 132 Filo looks after weapons and tactic training.* RENE VAN WOEZIK
Below: *A 171 Filo F-4E, armed with two Mk.83 bombs, sits on the ramp at Erhac.* RENE VAN WOEZIK

Phabulous Phantoms!

Retired or rare - some more stunning photos.

Above: *The US Navy was renowned for its colourfully painted Phantoms. F-4N 152277 of VF-111 'Sundowners' is a prime example, witness its American bicentennial tail markings, seen here at NAS Fallon on April 22, 1976.*

RENÉ FRANCILLON

Right: *Egypt is one of a number of Middle Eastern nations still flying the F-4 Phantom. Here a pair of Egyptian Air Force F-4Es overfly the Pyramids near Cairo.*

Below: *A pair of 'Recce Phantoms' in the shape of two 192nd FS RF-4Cs of the Nevada Air National Guard make an evocative sight over the barren Nevada landscape.*

PAUL CRICKMORE

Above: *The Test and Evaluation Squadron, VX-4, adorned one of its F-4s with this striking scheme to celebrate the American Bicentennial in 1976.* VIA RENÉ FRANCILLON

Above: *This immaculately turned out F-4EJ of Dai 306 Hiko-tai was based at Komatsu AB until the unit converted to the F-15J in 1997.* KATSUHIKO TOKUNAGA

Left: *Spain long since retired its F-4C Phantoms but this fine study of one of its camouflaged examples will bring back memories for some. Spain still operates a limited number of RF-4Cs at Torrejon with Ala 12.* DR STEFAN PETERSEN

This superbly posed shot of six 74 Squadron Phantom FGR.2s is more interesting than at first it might appear. If you look closely, you will see the aircraft are lined up so the tail codes read 'Tigers' – the unit being a member of the NATO Tiger Association. AFM - DUNCAN CUBITT

Direct to your door

Now is the time to take advantage of our special post-free* subscription offer for yourself or someone you know.

AirForces MONTHLY
airforcesmonthly.com
The World's Best Military Aviation Magazine

South East Asia Air Power Survey

USAF Special Operations

Ejection at Mach 2.6!

RAF in Saudi Arabia

AFM flies the Gripen

USAF Special Ops

AFM evaluates the Gripen

Ejection at Mach 2.6!

As a subscriber you will enjoy all of these benefits:

afm — **Post Free Delivery***
Convenient home delivery direct to your door at no additional cost.

afm — **Guaranteed Delivery**
You are guaranteed never to miss an issue. If your magazine is lost or damaged in the post we will replace it as long as it is within three months of its on-sale date at newsagents.

afm — **Early Delivery**
Each month your personal copy is despatched from our printers directly into the postal system so your copy should arrive before its on-sale date.

afm — **Price Guarantee**
The price stays the same for the chosen period of your subscription even if the cover cost should rise. And, as an extra bonus if you subscribe for two years there is a further saving of £5.00.

afm — **Money-back Guarantee**
Our money back guarantee means that, in the unlikely event you are not entirely satisfied, we will refund the remainder of your subscription.

Online Ordering
Now order online using our secure site at:
www.airforcesmonthly.com

USA and Canada
Readers in USA and Canada may place subscriptions by telephoning toll-free 800-688-6247 or by writing to AirForces Monthly, Key Publishing Ltd., PO Box 100, Avenel, NJ 07001.

AirForces Monthly Subscription

Please start my subscription with the...issue   PLEASE PRINT

Magazine delivery address
Name: _____
Address: _____
_____
Post town: _____
Country: _____ Post Code _____

Please debit my Mastercard, Eurocard, Visa

☐☐☐☐ ☐☐☐☐ ☐☐☐☐ ☐☐☐☐   Expires ☐☐ ☐☐

Please indicate registered name and address of credit card holder if different to above. All credit card transactions will be debited UK Sterling rate.
Send Coupon or photocopy to: Subscriptions Dept.,AirForces Monthly, Key Publishing Ltd., PO Box 300, Stamford, Lincs., PE9 1NA, United Kingdom.
Tel/24hr answer machine: (44)01780 480404, Fax 01780 757812, E-Mail: subs@keymags.co.uk, Online ordering: www.airforcesmonthly.com

	1 year	2 year
UK	☐ 35.40	☐ 65.80
EUROPE	☐ 41.10	☐ 77.20
USA	☐ 40.20 US$72.40	☐ 75.40 US$135.70
CANADA	☐ 44.40	☐ 83.80
ZONE 1	☐ 50.40	☐ 95.80
ZONE 2	☐ 52.20	☐ 99.40
SURFACE MAIL	☐ 41.10	☐ 72.20

Zone 1. Most of the world except Far East
Zone 2. Far East, Australia, New Zealand
*applies to UK delivery only

Methods of payment
Payment accepted by cheque, Postal Order, Credit Card (Mastercard, Eurocard and Visa) Giro (account no. 2147556) and US Dollar check (exchange rate £1.00 = US $1.80). If paying by credit card the charge will appear on your statement as Key Publishing Ltd.

Signature: ....   Offer expires June 30th 2000

On occasion Key Publishing make special offers on products or services that we believe to be of interest to our customers. If you do not wish to receive this information please tick here ☐

The Phantom
Drones On...

Two QF-4Es depart Tyndall for another mission. It takes just over four months to convert these aircraft from a retired has-been, to an important member of the 475th WEG at Tyndall AFB. ANDY JACOBUS

Although the Phantom is now just a memory in the active USAF inventory, former USAF examples continue to be drawn out of mothballs for conversion to full-scale aerial targets, as *AFM's* **Dave Allport reports from Mojave, California.**

SITUATED IN THE Mojave Desert, around 100 miles (160km) north of Los Angeles and west of Edwards AFB, the town of Mojave is little more than a small conglomeration at a crossroads in an otherwise dry, hot and largely unpopulated area of California. Mojave Airport, however, is home to several well-known aerospace companies, one of which is what was formerly Tracor Flight Systems Inc (TFSI). The company merged into GEC-Marconi's North American Group in June 1998 to become Marconi Flight Systems and more recently became the Flight Systems Inc division of BAE Systems Aeronautics in North America when British Aerospace completed its take-over of Marconi Electronic Systems on November 30, 1999. For the purpose of this article, we will continue to use the Tracor name, as this will be more familiar to most readers.

Tracor's Mojave operation is largely centred on conversion of surplus USAF Phantoms into QF-4 full-scale aerial targets, work currently underway being all from F-4Gs, although earlier examples included a fair number of F-4Es and a couple of RF-4Cs. At any one time, around nine aircraft are usually on the line undergoing conversion, with others on the apron either awaiting their turn or being prepared for delivery after completion.

Contracts

Tracor's first involvement in QF-4 conversions began with a February 1992 deal for a pre-production batch of ten aircraft.

Following successful completion of initial USAF operation, test and evaluation at Tyndall, Tracor was awarded a $18.1 million Lot 1 production contract on June 12, 1995, for 36 conversions – the first three of which were delivered to Tyndall in May 1996 with the last completed in May 1997. Lot 2 production, comprising a further 36 aircraft, followed on from this and the contract for the first element of Lot 3, covering modification of a further 24 aircraft, was awarded on October 20, 1997. A deal for the final element of Lot 3, comprising a

Phantoms on the ramp of the Aerospace Maintenance and Regeneration Center (AMARC) at Davis-Monthan AFB are pulled out of store and prepared for the short flight to Mojave. AFM-ALAN WARNES

Part of Tracor's QF-4 conversion line at Mojave on April 23, 1997, with four of the nine F-4Gs undergoing QF-4G conversion at the time visible. The three visible to the rear comprise two 'WW'-coded former Idaho ANG examples to the left and a 'WA'-coded former 57th Wing example to the right.
AFM-STEVE FLETCHER

further 12 aircraft, was finalised on April 17, 1998, and the last example was delivered in May 1999.

This was expected to be the final batch of QF-4s, bringing total conversions to 108, before an alternative airframe was selected for future conversions. However, on June 23, 1998, an $80 million follow-on production contract was awarded covering conversion of at least 72 and possibly as many as 192 more surplus F-4E/Gs over the following seven years to QF-4E/G full-scale aerial targets. The initial deal covered a firm order for 12 Lot 4 aircraft, which began delivery at the rate of one per month from June 1999, with the last examples currently being completed at Mojave. It also included options for a further five one-year production batches, each of which could comprise between 12-36 aircraft. The first of these options has now been exercised, with authorisation for 12 Lot 5 conversions being granted and first delivery from this batch due in mid-2000. Under the current production schedule, QF-4 deliveries will continue until 2006, when the last examples of Lot 9 are due to be completed.

AMARC

Most aircraft for conversion are now coming from desert storage at AMARC Davis-Monthan AFB although some earlier examples came direct from their last operational units, including around a dozen Wild Weasel F-4Gs from the Idaho ANG/124th FG/190th FS at Boise. Aircraft for conversion are selected by a small USAF/Air Force Materiel Command (AFMC) team, which chooses the low-time airframes, prepares them for delivery to Tracor and then flies them to Mojave using its own pilots. On completion, the aircraft are delivered, generally at the rate of three per month, making the two-day journey via Davis-Monthan AFB and either Holloman or Kelly AFBs to Tyndall AFB, Florida, to join the 475th WEG. Although not intended to be shot down until the end of their useful lives, the QF-4s will all ultimately be expended in this way — the first example was shot down at Tyndall around late March/early April 1997. In addition to operations from Tyndall, the aircraft are also

detached to Holloman AFB, New Mexico. As of January 3, 2000, some 218 F-4E/Gs remained 'in stock' at AMARC, all of these being potential candidates for QF-4 conversion, with many F-4Gs already earmarked for this work against the current contracts. (These are accompanied by 11 x F-4Cs, 17 x RF-4Bs, 17 x F-4Js, 24 x F-4Ns, 90 x F-4Ds, 142 x F-4S and 233 x RF-4Cs — for more on AMARC see *AFM's A Desert Treasure Trove*, February 98, p42-48.) Conversions of the F-4Es will then follow after the last of the F-4Gs have been converted. When these stocks are exhausted, an alternative type will have to be found, with consideration having already been given to drone conversions of the F-16 or A-4 Skyhawk.

Overall conversion of the Phantom to QF-4 configuration takes around $4\frac{1}{2}$ months per aircraft. On arrival at Mojave, the F-4s are given a visual acceptance inspection and then sit on the ramp, usually for around a month, to await their turn on the conversion line. Once

moved into the hangar, hydraulic and air systems are bled and the aircraft is stripped down; this process normally taking about a week. During the second week, mechanical and electrical modifications are undertaken, including installation of the servos and new electronics. Considerable rewiring is necessary because of all the additional equipment and various hydraulic systems are also replaced. The new equipment which will control the aircraft, manufactured by Lear, Sperry and Microsystems, is brought together as a package by Ogden Air Logistics Center at Hill AFB, Utah, and fitted in the aircraft on metal pallets made by Tracor. Thorough systems analysis and wiring verification is then undertaken over a four-week period. After five days of final systems testing, checking all flight controls, undercarriage and the like, the aircraft is weighed. Following dynamics testing at full military power, the aircraft is then painted. Aircraft retain their basic matt camouflage

'Self-destruct is only used as a last resort, due to the high cost of the airframe, and can only be activated on NOLO (no onboard live operator) missions.'

Above: *Detail shot of the wingtip of 475th WEG QF-4E 67-0390/AF-126 showing one of the six white scoring antennae and data relay units fitted to the aircraft – another is also visible protruding from the rear of the fin top.* AFM-DAVE ALLPORT

Right: *The gutted cockpit of an F-4G undergoing conversion.* AFM-STEVE FLETCHER

scheme on completion but the outer wing, outboard portion of the tailplane and the fin are painted a bright gloss red to aid conspicuity. After a functional check flight (FCF) by one of Tracor's two QF-4-rated pilots, the completed aircraft is delivered to Tyndall for acceptance checks by the USAF. If no problems are encountered, only one FCF of around 45-50 minutes is normally undertaken, including a Mach 1.6-1.8 run through the Edwards supersonic corridor.

Conversion

Two types of full-scale aerial targets are used by the USAF, described as 'Limited' and 'Unlimited', the former are airframes which are expected to have limited lives, with basic avionics and high-time engines and ballast replacing the radar in the nose. They will face live weapon attacks and are likely to be shot down sooner rather than later. The 'Unlimited' airframes will have lower hours and be fitted with a range of advanced defensive and offensive EW suites and/or threat emitter module systems. Such equipment is often highly sensitive and therefore is only installed by USAF personnel at Eglin and Tyndall, Tracor having no involvement in this work.

The conversion work includes installation of an additional autopilot, telemetry transponders (for both uplinking and downlinking information) in a fairing on the aircraft's spine, various antennae and servos to fly the aircraft (taking the place of pilot inputs with one each for throttle, rudder, pitch and aileron control). The throttle servos are installed in the port forward Sparrow missile recess, while circuit boards to encode and decode signals from the transponders are fitted in the gun port under the nose. An automatic flight control system is also installed, together with a flight termination system, the latter being necessary for any occasion when control is lost during unmanned operations. An Interim Vector Scoring System (IVSS) is installed to enable proximity assessment of a particular missile firing and relay to either another aircraft or ground station. Most firing is programmed for a 'near miss' of the aircraft, which is an expensive asset, thus the IVSS will still register a successful 'kill' if the weapon passes within a

few feet of the aircraft. Some shots, which are usually with telemetry rounds, rather than live warheads, may however hit the aircraft, and in this case the damage is assessed in flight to determine if the aircraft should be brought back for repair or destroyed using the self-destruct system. The charge from an AIM-9 warhead is fitted inside the aircraft (behind 'Door 16') for this purpose with a 'safe and arm' device actuated via a UHF destruct antenna. Once the command is received, the aircraft will move into a destruct orbit and blow itself up by firing the charge into the fuel system if no rescind command is transmitted. Self-destruct is only used as a last resort, due to the high cost of the airframe, and can only be activated on NOLO (no onboard live operator) missions.

The radar in the nose is normally still retained on the QF-4 although it is never used in the drone configuration, being merely retained for ballast. Externally, apart from the high-visibility paint, there is little to differentiate a QF-4 from any other Phantom. The only tell-tale signs being a small hump on top of the rear fuselage to house transponders and antennae switches, plus six white scoring antennae and data relay units. One appears on each of the wingtips, one protruding to the rear at the top of the fin, one each on top of and underneath the nose and another on the fuselage underside just aft of the intakes.

Conversion work is undertaken with the emphasis on minimum airframe changes in order that the aircraft can be easily de-converted back to its original configuration, although it is unlikely that this would take place. All systems are downlinked to ground stations for monitoring and the QF-4 is highly manoeuvrable, being fully supersonic and capable of a 4g barrel roll or 6g slice — in fact the aircraft flies much better without a pilot! In NOLO configuration the QF-4 can also undertake formation flying with up to four aircraft (the restriction on numbers being only because Tyndall's system cannot handle any more than this at the same time).

For normal operations the QF-4 is pre-programmed and needs little help from a ground controller, being capable of controlling itself sufficiently to line up on the centreline of the runway. Pilots are, however, used in order to maintain currency, check mission profiles and for control checks when he is almost literally 'just along for the ride' and will not touch the controls. Manned QF-4 operations at Tyndall are undertaken by Lockheed Martin

pilots under contract to the USAF, but they have all been trained by Tracor.

Tracor is also one of few civilian companies to have air refuelling-qualified pilots, who are very hard to come by now. This resulted in the company obtaining the contract to ferry Egyptian Air Force F-4E Phantoms to and from the USA to undergo PDMs at NADep Cherry Point, North Carolina. However, it is now unlikely that any further such flights will be made as Tracor has become increasingly concerned that the aircraft are no longer in a good enough condition to undertake such long ferry flights. This viewpoint was substantiated in 1994 when two Egyptian F-4Es were abandoned at RAF Lakenheath for nearly four months before technicians could make them sufficiently airworthy for their onward journey to the USA.

Tracor Fleet

Tracor also operates its own fleet of 18 ex-military high-performance jet aircraft, one of the largest such privately-operated fleets in the world, which are used for trials work and to fulfil a variety of other contracts. The fleet includes four F-4D Phantom IIs which are on loan from the USAF and replaced Tracor's earlier F-4Cs (also loaned from the USAF). Of the four, two are used for general trials work, whilst the other two are dedicated to the US Navy as launch vehicles for Beechcraft AQM-37C air-launched expendable targets, continuing trials work started with the earlier F-4Cs. These liquid-fuelled rocket targets are normally launched from an LAU-24 trapeze ejector on the F-4Ds at Mach 1.5 and 50,000ft (15,240m) and feature both radar and IR augmentation.

TRACOR F-4D PHANTOM II TRIALS FLEET

N424FS ex USAF/64-0965, arrived Mojave March 28, 1991
N426FS ex USAF/65-0763, arrived March 19, 1991
N427FS ex USAF/66-7505, arrived August 14, 1991
N430FS ex USAF/66-7483, arrived September 24, 1991

Using a preset guidance programme, the basic version is capable of achieving speeds of up to Mach 3 and altitudes of 80,000ft (24,385m), although a developed variant is capable of Mach 4 and 100,000ft (30,480m). Tracor's F-4Ds are also used for weapons drop trials on behalf of manufacturers, most of this work being R&D on advanced guided weapons. Although much of Tracor's work in this field involves captive flights some live firing is also undertaken.

F-4D N424FS is one of four used by Tracor for a wide variety of trials work. AFM-DAVE ALLPORT

Two 69 Sqn 'Hammers' F-4E Phantoms in close formation. The unit now operates F-15Is.

Thirty years of Constant Hammering

Shlomo Aloni **looks at the career of the Israeli Phantom.**

THIRTY YEARS of service with the Israel Defence Force/Air Force (IDF/AF) earned the McDonnell Douglas F-4E Phantom the well-deserved reputation of being a hard-worker. Despite the purchase of much more sophisticated fighters in recent years and the hopes for peace in the Middle East, it is still just speculation to try to foresee when the awesome Kurnass (Sledgehammer) will disappear from the skies on which it stamped such a glorious piece of aerial history.

Multi-role was a well-known IDF/AF slogan for many years, but it was given a new meaning when the McDonnell Douglas F-4E Phantom entered IDF/AF service in 1969. For the first time in its history, the IDF/AF possessed a fighter-bomber that really had the ability and performance to realise the IDF/AF concept of a multi-role fighter. Until then, the IDF/AF had

The distinctive lines of the Phantom. An IDF/AF F-4E equipped with four Rafael Shafrir air-to-air missiles and the fixed air refuelling probe.

either operated attack aircraft with limited air-to-ground capability or fighters with limited air-to-air capability. The F-4E introduced for the first time a platform which was equally good in both missions.

Service Entry

Two squadrons were formed on the type in 1969 after ten aircrews – six pilots and four navigators – had converted on the type with the 4452nd Tactical Fighter Training School (TFTS) at George AFB, California. Those ten comprised an elite team – they were to form the skeleton of the two units and were seen by many as the next generation commanders of the IDF/AF; a promise they fulfilled. Of those top ten pilots and navigators one, Avihu Ben-Nun, became the IDF/AF commander (1987-1992), and two others retired from the IDF/AF as Brigadier Generals. Combat also took its toll on the group, though, with three members bring killed in action (KiA) and another four enduring the suffering of Prisoners of War (PoW).

The first unit, 201 Sqn known as 'The One Squadron', was formed at Hatzor on August 17, 1969, with Maj Shmuel Hetz in command, and the first four Kurnass aircraft arrived at Hatzor on September 5 following a delivery flight from the US. Operations commenced almost immediately: at first the three pilots and two navigators of the second squadron flew with 201 Sqn. Then 69 Sqn, known as 'The Hammers', was formed at Ramat-David on October 23, 1969, with Maj Avihu Ben-Nun in command.

The first local conversion course began in September 1969, first with 201 Sqn and then with 69 Sqn. It included eleven pilots (including the first IDF/AF ace Capt Giora Rom, who was shot down over Egypt on September 11, became a PoW, and was replaced in the conversion course by Capt Ig'al Shochat, who later became a PoW himself) and seven navigators. Meanwhile, 69 Sqn combat-rated aircrews flew operations with 201 Sqn. The two squadron commanders performed a two-ship formation supersonic boom over Cairo on November 4. On November 11, another mixed

two-ship formation resulted in the first Kurnass air-to-air kill when an Egyptian Air Force (EAF) MiG-21 was shot down by a 69 Sqn crew, Capt Ehud Henkin and Maj Achicar Eyal, in a 201 Sqn Kurnass 608. Six days later the first combat loss occurred when 201 Sqn attacked a radar station at Jordan. Maj Ehud Henkin and Lt Shaul Levi of 69 Sqn, flying in 201 Sqn Kurnass 604, were shot down by anti-aircraft (AA) fire and ejected safely over friendly territory.

The first operational sortie of 69 Sqn on November 28 marked an almost incredible achievement. In just over two months since the arrival of the first four examples, the IDF/AF brought to operational status two Kurnass squadrons which had already performed a wide variety of missions, including the common Combat Air Patrol (CAP), Battlefield Air Interdiction (BAI) and Suppression of Enemy

Above: *After years of being an air defence fighter, Israel's F-4Es now fulfill an air-to-ground role, as portrayed by this 'Bats' Sqn F-4E in full afterburner.* ALL PICTURES IAF UNLESS STATED

Left: *The IDFA/F operate three F-4E (S) including this example, serialled 499 which features an enlarged nose and a HIAC-1 camera which rotates to view from any of the four windows. Meanwhile the vertically mounted KS-87 camera is evident in thois photograph.* AMOS DOR/IAF AIRCRAFT SERIES

Air Defence (SEAD) as well as such bizarre missions as performing supersonic booms over the enemy's major cities. They also claimed the first air-to-air kill and suffered the first combat loss.

It was an extraordinary achievement, even for the combat-proven IDF/AF and was followed by even more daring highlights in 1970. In the first quarter, the IDF/AF Kurnass ranged all over Egypt in a long series of deep penetration strikes, which only came to an end when the USSR deployed to Egypt a complete air defence division. Having succeeded in deterring the IDF/AF from launching the Kurnass deep into Egypt, the Soviets started to 'roll' the air defence network forward towards the Suez Canal and the IDF/AF Kurnass community suffered heavily when five aircraft were lost in the summer of 1970 during SEAD missions over Egypt. Of the ten aircrews involved, one navigator was retrieved from enemy territory by an IDF/AF helicopter, seven became PoWs and two were killed, including 201 Sqn's CO, Major Shmuel Hetz. A kind of revenge was achieved on July 30 when in a well-planned ambush, five Soviet MiG-21s were shot down, including two by 69 Sqn. Days later, on August 3, a ceasefire came into effect, and the Attrition War was over – but not IDF/AF Kurnass operations.

Expansion and Shock

The end of the Attrition War allowed the IDF/AF to form a third Kurnass outfit under the command of Lt Col Amos Amir in the shape of 119 Sqn, known as 'The Bat Squardon', which accepted its first six Kurnass aircraft at Tel-Nof on October 29, 1970. The fourth unit to be formed was 107 Sqn, known as 'The Orange

'Highly-praised Kurnass aircrews were the ones who succeeded in fulfilling their missions, sometimes against all odds, rather than those crews who claimed air-to-air kills.'

	KNOWN ISRAELI YOM KIPPUR WAR KURNASS LOSSES				
Date	AA	SAM	AA or SAM	Enemy a/c	Remarks
06/10	-	1	-	-	2 KIA
07/10	-	1	6	-	2 KIA, 11 PoW[1], 2 retrieved
08/10	-	2	3	1	4 KIA, 2 PoW, 6 retrieved
09/10	-	-	2	-	1 KIA, 1 PoW, 2 retrieved
10/10	-	-	-	-	
11/10	1	-	1	2	2 KIA, 4 PoW, 2 retrieved
12/10	1	-	-	-	2 retrieved
13/10	-	-	1	-	4 retrieved[2]
14/10	-	-	-	-	2 retrieved[3]
15/10	-	1	-	-	1 KIA, 1 PoW, 2 retrieved[4]
16/10	-	-	-	-	
17/10	-	-	1	-	2 KIA
18/10	-	-	2	-	4 PoW
19/10	-	-	-	-	
20/10	-	2	-	-	2 PoW, 2 retrieved
21/10	-	-	-	1	1 KIA, 1 PoW
22/10	-	-	-	-	
23/10	-	-	-	-	
24/10	-	-	-	-	
TOTAL	2	7	16	4	Plus 3 a/c lost to other causes, see notes.
Notes	1	One navigator ejected to become PoW but pilot landed in Israel.			
	2	One a/c lost to technical malfunction.			
	3	One a/c lost to 'friendly fire'.			
	4	One a/c shot down by a 'friendly' Nesher.			

Above: *The Rafael Python 3 air-to-air missile was introduced into service by the 'Hammers' Sqn in 1978.* IDF/AF VIA SHLOMO ALONI

Below: *The emphasis on the mission accomplishment 'myth' rather than on air-to-air kills resulted in this post-1982 Lebanon War attempt to decorate the Kurnass with SAM kill markings. Kurnass 317 carries two such markings.* SHLOMO ALONI

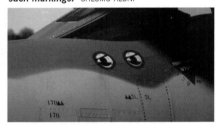

ISRAELI KURNASS CHRONOLOGY

Year	Known combat losses	Known losses to accidents	Known air-to-air kills	Remarks
1969	1	-	1	'The One Sqn' & 'The Hammers Sqn' are formed
1970	6	1	7	The Attrition War ends, The 'Bat Sqn' is formed
1971	-	-	-	
1972	-	2	4	
1973	33	-	100	The 'Orange Tail Knights Sqn' formed. The Yom Kippur War
1974	2	1	2	
1975	-	1	-	The 'Scorpion Sqn' formed
1976	-	1	-	
1977	-	3	-	
1978	-	1	-	Operation LITANI, Lebanon
1979	-	1	-	
1980	-	-	0.5	
1981	-	2	-	
1982	1	-	2	The Lebanon War
1983	-	-	-	
1984	-	3	-	
1985	-	-	-	
1986	1	-	-	The 'Scorpion Sqn' disbanded
1987	-	-	-	
1988	-	-	-	The 'One Sqn' transferred to Tel-Nof
1989	-	1	-	Kurnass 2000 enters service
1990	-	-	-	
1991	-	1	-	The 'Hammers Sqn' transferred to Hatzerim
1992	-	-	-	
1993	-	-	-	
TOTAL	**44**	**18**	**116.5**	

REMARK: The figures quoted here are only 'known' numbers and not official statistics. Statistics for the last six years have not been approved for publication

Tail Knights', which was formed at Hatzerim in late-1973, shortly before the Yom Kippur War, with Lt Col Iftach Spector in command.

The four Kurnass squadrons operating out of four air bases became the central core of Israeli air power. As such, they went from strength to strength until October 6, 1973, when the Yom Kippur War broke out and they had to perform the costly Suppression of Enemy Air Defence (SEAD) mission while also performing any imaginable scenario of combat flying. The 19-day war cost the IDF/AF Kurnass community dearly. In the course of more than 3,000 operational sorties, over 30 aircraft were lost, many of the aircrews either being KiA or becoming PoWs. Of the four Kurnass units, 201 Sqn suffered the heaviest number of losses. Thirteen of its aircraft were lost, with six of the aircrews KiA and another 13 becoming PoWs.

As the war was about to break out on October 6, the IDF/AF was preparing for a pre-emptive strike, which ultimately was not approved by the Israeli Government. The Arab offensive was launched at noon, giving the IDF/AF only a few daylight hours to dispatch its aircraft in a frantic attempt to support the hard-pressed IDF ground forces. During those few hours, the Kurnass were credited with at least 22 air-to-air kills. A single Kurnass was lost to either anti-aircraft (AA) fire or to a surface-to-air missile (SAM) during an attack on the bridges the Egyptian army had constructed across the Suez Canal.

Although the first day of the war was a relative success for the Kurnass community, October 7 – the first full day of fighting – was the day which shook the foundations of the IDF/AF. In the early hours of the morning, the IDF/AF launched Operation TAGAR (Haggle) to achieve air superiority over Egypt. However, when the aircraft returned from the first wave, the aircrews learnt that the operation was called off and that a new effort, Operation DOOGMAN 5 (Model 5), was to be launched to suppress the Syrian air defence network. Once again, only one wave was flown, and the operation was called off when the IDF/AF command learnt of the number of losses sustained in this first wave. Five Kurnass were lost and another two damaged examples made emergency landings at Ramat-David. From one of these aircraft, the pilot walked away alone – the navigator had ejected over Syria to become a PoW. The IDF/AF estimated that only a single Syrian SAM battery had been destroyed. With such an unthinkable exchange rate, the operation was called off.

Another two bad days for the IDF/AF Kurnass squadrons were October 11 and 13. On October 11, a 201 Sqn formation was surprised on its way back home by Egyptian MiG-21s, with the loss of two aircraft. On October 13, Lt Col Iftach Zemer, the squadron commander, had to eject following a technical malfunction, and suffered a back injury. He was succeeded by Maj Eitan Ben-Eliyahu, the current IDF/AF commander (it is interesting to note that the nominated successor of Maj Gen Ben-Eliyahu as IDF/AF commander is Maj Gen Dan Halotz, who also flew as a reservist with 201 Sqn during the Yom Kippur War).

Apart from the heavy losses and the frustration caused by the failure to achieve total air superiority of the kind the Israeli aircrews aspired to, the Kurnass squadrons performed well during the war: in the dangerous air-to-ground arena and also in the rather more glamorous air-to-air missions, with almost 100 confirmed kills.

A New Role for the Old War Horses

Following the war, the IDF/AF Kurnass continued operations. A recce Kurnass was lost over Egypt on November 9, 1973, and the spring of 1974 brought a short but bitter confrontation with Syria over the control of Mount Hermon. This ended with the IDF in control of this highly-important strongpoint, though it also cost the IDF/AF another two of its precious Kurnasses.

The fifth IDF/AF Kurnass unit, 105 Sqn (known as 'The Scorpion Squardon'), was formed on March 31, 1975. By this time, the US-negotiated talks which followed the Yom Kippur War resulted in a US arms package to Israel which included the first batch of the F-15

A Phantom is towed back to its heavily camouflaged revetment area.

A fascinating photo of a Kurnass chasing an Egyptian Air Force MiG-17 on October 7, 1973.

Eagle, and the purchase of the F-16 Fighting Falcon was to be finalised before the decade was over. This marked the end of the glorious days for the Kurnass and a new role had to be found for the old war horses.

Right from the start, the Kurnass was viewed as a true multi-role combat aircraft and since its aircrews had to excel in so many missions, the IDF/AF command did not emphasise excellence in a single mission. Hence the Kurnass, except for a few rare occasions, did not carry air-to-air kill markings as did other IDF/AF aircraft. While air-to-air kills could not be discarded, it was felt that the successful fulfilment of a mission was the true scale by which to judge the aircrews. Highly-praised Kurnass aircrews were the ones who succeeded

in fulfilling their missions, sometimes against all odds, rather than those crews who claimed air-to-air kills. This was further emphasised in the late 1970s and early 1980s, when the F-15 and F-16 entered IDF/AF service and the primary mission of the Kurnass became air-to-ground attack.

This shift was demonstrated in the June 1982 Lebanon War during which the Kurnass mainly flew attack missions, excelling in particular at destroying the Syrian air defence network in the Lebanon Valley. Two Kurnass aircrews were decorated for successfully destroying SAM batteries, and the aircraft adorned with SAM-kill markings. As a bonus, the Kurnass scored its last air-to-air kill on June 11, 1982, an occasion which was also the first kill for 105

Sqn as a Kurnass unit.

A Striker for the Next Millennium

In the 1980s, the Kurnass community witnessed two parallel processes: running down and streamlining of the force as opposed to a new upgrade programme: the Kurnass 2000. The Kurnass 2000 programme was aimed at giving the aircraft a new lease of life as a dedicated all-weather strike aircraft and two squadrons commenced to receive the Kurnass 2000 in 1989. The current Kurnass 2000 squadrons are vastly more capable than the 1969 counterparts: they also rely heavily on a proud heritage accumulated in over 30 years of constant combat flying.

author's note

Squadron numbers are based on many previously-published public sources, such as:

1. Books. For example, Peter Mersky's 'Israeli Fighter Aces' (Speciality Press, 1997). Mersky was generously assisted by several senior IDF/AF officers, so his book can be viewed as a reliable semi-official source.
2. Internet sites such as www.flight2000.com/hangar/ aeroflight/ waf/israel by John Hayles.
3. The press, including Israeli newspapers which, on rare occasions, do publish IDF/AF squadron numbers.

IDF/AF Operational Phantom units

201 Sqn 'The One Sqn' – Sept 69-present

69 Sqn 'The Hammers Sqn' – Nov 69-Feb94

119 Sqn 'The Bat Sqn' – Nov 70-present

107 Sqn 'The Knights of the Orange Tail Sqn' – Dec 71-not current

105 Sqn 'The Scorpion Sqn' – Mar 75-1986

ALL DRAWINGS - AMOS DOR/IAF AIRCRAFT SERIES

Israel Air Force Phantom air-crews are among the most combat-proven in the world.
AFM-ALAN WARNES

Israel's
Warriors

AFM's Alan Warnes recently travelled to Tel Aviv to meet Lt Col (ret) David Yair, a navigator on Phantoms who was shot down twice during the formative years of the Phantom in Israel DF/AF service. He also talked to Colonel (ret) Amnon Gurion, a former F-4 pilot credited with two air-to-air kills.

DAVID YAIR

BORN IN 1944, David Yair grew up at kibbutz Gvar'am. In August 1962 he was recruited into Flying Course No.43 but 'washed out'. After serving as a paratrooper, he then returned to the flying school and graduated as a navigator in 1967. For a year he served as a navigator on the Nord Noratlas, then transferred to the Vautour. He was chosen as one of the elite ten under the command of Major Schmuel Hetz, to convert to the Phantom (or Kurnass in Israeli service) with the USAF's 4452nd TFTS at George AFB, California, from March 1969 to August 1969. David returned to Israel to join 'The One Sqn' and completed his first F-4 Kurnass combat mission on October 22, 1969. He was shot down twice during his Kurnass career. He flew approximately 250 combat missions in the Phantom (which included three air-to-air kills – two MiG-21s and a helicopter). He is reluctant to discuss these, but admits to one in the Attrition War and another during the Yom Kippur War.

In 1972 he left the IDF/AF to undertake a BSc aerospace engineering course, which was interrupted in 1973 when he returned to service to take part in the Yom Kippur War. He completed the course in 1977 and then spent five years with the IDF/AF Flight Test Centre as Chief Engineer. In 1982 he returned to the air as a navigator in F-15s just before the Lebanon War broke out. He retired as a Lieutenant Colonel in 1984 having completed 40 combat F-15 sorties. Today he works in the aerospace industry.

The Phantom according to David

David has nothing but praise for the Phantom. "During the War of Attrition we owed the survival of Israel to the Kurnass. While the F-15 is an easy aircraft to fly and fight with — as we proved against Syria in the 1982 Lebanon War when we had 85 air-to-air kills to their none. In the War of Attrition you felt that if you lost this battle it could be the last one. The Phantom was a tool with which we needed to survive."

He believes the Phantom changed the IAF's parameters. Its arrival in 1969 was a revelation. In the air-to-air mission it was as efficient as other aircraft in the region, for example the MiG-21, but where it really made the difference was in the air-to-ground role – no other aircraft could match it.

"Our Skyhawks could drop bombs with its computerised navigation system, but it could not mix it with the MiGs. In the Phantom we could put it in every mission. For me, the Phantom proved its worth in the air-to-ground configuration. It could fly fast, at low levels loaded with bombs; then if necessary, you could open up your afterburners and after 45 seconds, you could be at 20,000 feet.

"The French aircraft and Skyhawks we had operated prior to the Phantom, climbed very slowly, which would make easy pickings for the MiGs. If you went long distances you would need an escort – this was not a requirement with the Phantom. During the Yom Kippur War, we shot down MiG-21s, with most of the fights emanating from air-to-ground missions in their territory. You cannot say that it was only the pilots that made the difference... it was the Phantom."

The ejections

"On June 30, 1970, during the War of Attrition, Itzhak Peer my pilot and I were in Kurnass No.80 and on an air-to-ground mission over Egypt — our target being a SAM site. We came under attack from anti-aircraft artillery and 'Strela' shoulder-launched missiles.

"However, at about 45 minutes before sunset, and with a lot of haze in the sky, two missiles coming in from the west hit us — they had been impossible to see as they came at us from the direction of the sun. We decided to carry on but the damaged aircraft was then hit by a third. I believe it was two SA-2s and an SA-3.

"We ejected over the west bank of the Suez Canal. I was under the canopy for about 10-15 minutes and during this time Egyptian soldiers captured my pilot, who had landed close to the crashed aircraft. [Itzhak Peer was held by Egypt as a prisoner of war until November 1973.] Although I could not see him, I was aware of the unfolding situation on my radio, which I had been talking into as I drifted down to earth.

"An Egyptian soldier opened chase and nearly caught me, but I ran very fast and escaped. Later, I remembered I had hurt my knee playing football the previous day, which had required me needing some help to get into the aircraft on this mission. I had forgotten all about it!

"Having found a place to hide I waited for approximately 7-8 hours for the rescue helicopter. As it came in, there was tremendous ground fire. There were five personnel on board, two pilots, a flight engineer and two soldiers. I knew one of the pilots and shouted to him, 'I knew that you would come'.

He responded 'We did not know – you landed in the heart of the Egyptian Army'. In my view it was crazy to do it. In later years, I found out that when General Haim Bar-Lev, Chief of the Army at the time, and who had filled a number of top military jobs, was quizzed as to what his hardest decision was, he admitted that it had been this rescue mission.

"That day another Kurnass had gone down half an hour earlier in the same area, so there had been four people to rescue. He had been advised that there was no real chance of getting us out but that only he could decide whether to give the go-ahead for the rescue attempt.

"It is very important for a pilot at war to think that no effort will be spared to rescue him. You need to believe that the IAF would not leave you out there – it encapsulates the great spirit within the force. Two days after being rescued, I nervously climbed into a Kurnass for another mission.

"On October 13, 1973, during the Yom Kippur War, I experienced my second ejection, this time from Kurnass No.18. My pilot and I were en route to attack an airfield close to Damascus, Syria, but with nothing going to plan, we decided to return to base. However, as we started to turn back, we had a change of mind and continued our mission. As we went into a dive, on the outskirts of Damascus, we came under heavy fire from AAA and a few SA-6 missiles. Unfortunately we received a direct hit, from AAA probably no larger than 20mm. "I believe it hit the aircraft in the area of the main fuel tank, as the gauge reading showed there was 12,000lbs of fuel left, but by the time we had reached the Lebanese

coast, it was down to zero and there were flames underneath the aircraft. We ejected over the coastline at about six o'clock, on a very cold morning, but were not sure whether we would land on the ground or in the sea.

"As we descended, our wingman circled us, but there were people on the ground shooting, so I grabbed my radio and told him to leave. We eventually fell into the sea and the firing continued, approximately 200 metres away from our position. My pilot and I climbed into our dinghy. The people on the shore started to climb into a boat and head out to us, but were stopped when one of the formating IAF aircraft patrolling our position opened fire on it. Surprisingly, it kept missing. I later found out from the pilot that this was intentional, because if he had hit the boat and killed someone, it was unlikely that we would have survived any capture. "After approximately 70 minutes in the water, our rescue helicopter, a Bell 205 picked us up and dropped us off at a base in the north. However, we found ourselves standing on a ramp with no one around. We had been in the water so we were suffering from the cold, and my pilot had suffered injuries to his legs, so I took him on my shoulders and walked to the nearest telephone. I rang the medical centre and they sent someone out to pick us up. I was surprised to find that I had broken two ribs. It was all a far cry from my rescue in Egypt, when a reception had been waiting for us when we returned to base!

> **"During the War of Attrition we owed the survival of Israel to the Kurnass."**

AMNON GURION

BORN IN 1946, Amnon Gurion grew up at kibbutz Bet-Ha'shita, and graduated from the Israel Air Force Pilots School on Flying Course No.50 in July 1966. He flew Ouragans from 1966 to 1967, which included 17 sorties during the Six Day War. Amnon served as a flying school Instructor, prior to becoming one of the first pilots to convert to the Kurnass in 1969, on Conversion Course No.3. He flew with 'The One Sqn' under the command of Major Schmuel Hetz, who was sadly killed on July 18, 1970. During the 1973 Yom Kippur War, he served as Junior Deputy Commander to Major Eitan Ben-Eliahu (the current Israel Air Force Commander), while the Senior Deputy Commander then was Major Ron Holdai (current Mayor of Tel Aviv). Amnon flew 38 combat sorties, and was credited with two operational air-to-air kills – a Syrian Air Force MiG-21 on November 21, 1972 and an Egyptian Air Force MiG-21 on March 1, 1973. In 1977 he became a Nesher Squadron Commander and converted the unit to Kfirs during 1977-78. (Some of these Neshers were later upgraded by IAI and sold to Argentina, which subsequently used them during the Falklands War.) In 1979 Amnon was promoted to the Head of Aircraft Branch, Operational Requirements and from 1980-82 he studied at the US Air Warfare College at Maxwell AFB. Returning to Israel, he converted to F-15s and was promoted to Colonel, serving as the first Vice Commander of Tel Nof AB between 1984-85. In 1986 he was posted to the Head of the HQ Training Department and retired as a Colonel in 1988.

Today he works in the aerospace industry.

Those air-to-air kills

On November 21, 1972, while on a Kurnass mission over Syria, Amnon found himself in an aerial battle involving 18 IAF Mirages and Kurnasses against approximately 24 MiG-21s. He was No.3, leading a second pair, and accompanying him as navigator was Lt Baruch Golan (who was later killed in the Yom Kippur War). Amnon takes up the story of the battle: "The sun was low and when you were dogfighting in these conditions the MiG-21s were clearly distinct from the Mirage and Kurnass because when afterburning in a manoeuvre, they would leave four or five rings trailing behind them. We started the fight at 30-35,000 feet and I was chasing a MiG-21, and hitting him with bullets from my cannon, but nothing was happening — the aircraft just would not explode. However at about 5,000 feet, while we were pulling about 4-6gs, I fired at him again but was not sure I had hit him until my colleagues confirmed the loss, and that the pilot had ejected. All the time my navigator had been watching my tail."

On his second air-to-air kill, Amnon was on a patrolling recce mission, with Lt Itzhak Amitai as his navigator, over Egypt.

"At about 7-10,000 feet, while flying approximately 550 knots, I encountered a MiG and the chase was on. I chased him and he manoeuvred sharply... he went down low over the coast of the Gulf of Suez. At times, I could almost see the eyes of the pilot — we were that close. I pushed on into a scissors manoeuvre,

and as he got down closer to the water, he tried to recover at low speed. At this point, I pulled my flaps up and launched a Deker IR [AIM-9D Sidewinder] air-to air missile and because of his very low speed and thrust he could not manoeuvre to avoid it. The explosion was very close and the aircraft fell into the water like a leaf. "In a dogfight, you feel something very special and it's done by instinct. Afterwards I thought that I should have done it differently and perhaps I might have got more than one. It's a natural reaction I think. You have to be ready to take a risk and to be enthusiastic about what you are doing."

Col (Ret) Amnon Gurion, is accredited with two air-to-air kills during the Yom Kippur War.
AFM-ALAN WARNES

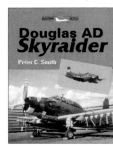
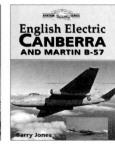

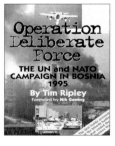

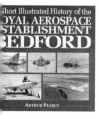

German
evolution

Andreas Klein looks at the service career of Luftwaffe Phantoms.

An RF-4E of AkG 52 from Leck over northern Germany with undercarriage and arrester hook down.
DR STEFAN PETERSEN

ON JANUARY 20, 1971, a new era began for the Luftwaffe when the first McDonnell Douglas F-4 Phantom II was handed over to Aufklarungsgeschwader (AkG – Reconnaissance Wing) 51 at Bremgarten AB. The first four of 88 RF-4Es ordered had been delivered via Torrejon in Spain and Ramstein in Germany, where the USAF insignias were removed and all four RF-4Es received the same German tactical code 35+01 (in case one aircraft broke down en-route). However, there was to be a long wait before the Phantom could enter German Air Force (GAF) service.

In the early 1950s, NATO was outnumbered by Warsaw Pact forces, and to counter this imbalance, NATO's higher echelons introduced

doctrines MC 14/1 and 14/2, Massive Retaliation. These meant that any military attack on NATO territory would be stopped by the immediate use of nuclear weapons. Firepower for these attacks would have been provided by platforms operating from mainland USA, well out of the reach of Soviet nuclear weapons. The tactical and strategic aim was to wipe out the enemy immediately.

This strategic advantage came to a sudden end on October 10, 1957, when Sputnik, the world's first satellite, was sent into earth's orbit and proved to the Western world that Russia was capable of providing a powerful carrier system for their nuclear forces. This stalemate meant that the dangers of a nuclear holocaust continued to threaten the world throughout the following decades. In the early 1960s, NATO officials came up with a new concept: NATO would regain flexibility in the usage of its power and overcome the old dilemma 'all or nothing'. These ideas led to NATO doctrine MC 14/3 Flexible Response. The policy of deterrence remained the main objective, though any possible threat would be countered with appropriate measures on a very low level of escalation. Every NATO member, Germany included, had to make a contribution – a decision which led to a complete change in the tactical duties and training of NATO's flying wings from strike to conventional attacks.

The F-104G Starfighter formed the backbone of the GAF in the mid-1960s. Equipped with an old radar and insufficient air-to-air and air-to-ground capabilities for the duties to come, it also lacked the necessary performance to support MC 14/3, and it soon became obvious

Above: *A fully-armed F-4F of JG 74 carrying four AIM-9L Sidewinders and AIM-120 AMRAAMs.*
AUTHOR

Left: *A JG 71 'Richthofen' F-4F ICE armed with four AIM-9L Sidewinders heads for the heavens at dusk.* DR STEFAN PETERSEN

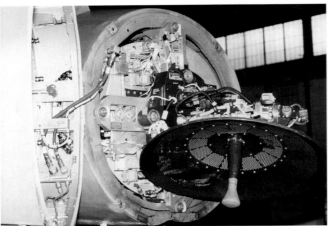

Above left: *The AN/APQ-120-V-5 radar is used in the 43 F-4F ICE variants that received the first two stages of a three-stage upgrade. They are referred to as air-to-ground aircraft, and are easily distinguishable by their black noses.* AUTHOR

Above right: *The 113 F-4F ICE variants that received the full three-stage upgrade are referred to as the air defence variant. These aircraft had their AN/APQ-120-V-5 radars replaced by the superior AN/APG-65GY radar seen here and sport a grey nose.* AUTHOR

to the German Department of Defence that this aircraft had to be replaced. The new tactics increased the demand and importance of reconnaissance assets. While using nuclear weapons, precision during the delivery process could be neglected, but to fight an enemy conventionally, it is necessary to know its location, even deep within its own country. It was decided to begin the anticipated replacements of GAF aircraft with the RF-104G to counter a so-called recce gap. The much better suited RF-4E was chosen as its successor.

In May 1968, Germany placed an order for 88 RF-4Es worth DM2.1 billion. Major changes had to be made to the infrastructure on the German bases in order to introduce this aircraft, such as new and bigger aircraft shelters. In addition, because of the need for a second aircrew member and the increased complexibility of the F-4 during the maintenance process, the 1,650 personnel required by a standard F-104 unit had to be increased to 1,925. New simulators also had to be imported from the US, and on arrival, the F-4 underwent a thorough inspection, while the ejection seats were exchanged. All the aircraft were divided between AkG 51 'Immelmann'

stationed at Bremgarten in southern Germany, and AkG 52 stationed at Leck in the north. One RF-4E (serialled 35+62) was sent to Technical School 1 (TsLw 1) at Kaufbeuren to train ground crews, and 35+01 (later redesignated 98+01) was used by Test and Evaluation Centre 61 (WTD 61) at Manching.

The German Phantoms were all delivered by USAF crews, and only became the responsibility of the Germans once they had arrived at Bremgarten. By June 1972, RF-4Es had replaced all the RF-104Gs. During the late 1970s and early 1980s, the RF-4Es were upgraded to carry 5,000lb (2,268kg) of conventional armament, and a visor was added to the front cockpit. After the reunification of Germany, the German Department of Defence agreed to a reduction of forces as laid down in the so-called Four Plus Two treaties – up to approximately 250 aircraft were affected, which led to the withdrawal of all Alphajets and RF-4Es. Withdrawal began with AkG 51 'I', which was disbanded in 1992, and continued with AkG 52, which closed down in 1994. Twenty-seven Phantoms were sold to Greece and 46 to Turkey. The last remaining RF-4E in Luftwaffe service is 35+62, used to train F-4F ground crews at TsLw 1 at

Kaufbeuren, and which will eventually be handed over to the Luftwaffe Museum at Berlin-Gatow in 2002 or 2003.

Meanwhile, in August 1971, the German Government — satisfied with the RF-4E Phantom — authorised the purchase of 175 F-4Fs in the interceptor and fighter-bomber role, at a cost of DM4 billion. First flight of the F-4F took place on March 18, 1973, with roll out on March 24. Deliveries went ahead in 1973, around 12 aircraft from the initial batch going directly to the 35th TFW at George AFB, California, to train German air crews. Flight crew training began on January 1, 1974, with crews from Jagdgeschwader 71 (JG - Fighter Wing) 'Richthofen', the first unit to receive the F-4F for operational use. The first F-4F to arrive on German soil, however, was 37+04 which, together with 37+14, went directly to the GAF Technical School for ground crew training, where these two aircraft still serve. The second unit to trade in its ageing Starfighters was JG 74 'Mölders', stationed at Neuburg, Bavaria.

Replacements began early in 1974 and ended in 1975. JG 74 was followed by Jagdbombergeschwader (JbG - Fighter Bomber Wing) 36 at Rheine-Hopsten, and lastly by JbG 35, when as Leichtes Kampfgeschwader (LekG - Light Attack Wing) 42 it traded in its Fiat G-91 aircraft. The introduction of the F-4F ended on October 10, 1976, with the delivery of 38+75, *Spirit of Co-operation*, to JbG 35, based at Pferdsfeld, and the handover of 37+15, 37+16 and 38+13 to WTD 61. So that the F-4Fs at George could be used with combat units, ten F-4Es were bought as replacements in 1977. These aircraft, serialled 75-0628 to 75-0637, were more compatible with the F-4 in USAF use, and together with other 20th FS aircraft, were used to train GAF pilots and Weapons Systems Operators (WSOs). To distinguish the GAF and USAF F-4Es, the former wore German national colours on their fin tips. Three F-4Es were lost: 75-0634 and 75-0637 collided on November 21, 1983, while 75-0630 crashed on July 26, 1990, after entering an unrecoverable flat spin. All the other F-4Es were phased out in 1997, and were replaced by F-4Fs.

JG 71 'Richthofen' was declared combat-ready again in 1974 and JG 74 'Mölders' in 1975. Their primary mission was air defence,

Above: *The pilot's front cockpit in an F-4F ICE.*
AUTHOR

Right: *The Weapons System Operator's office. As you can see, there is restricted forward view.* AUTHOR

with a secondary air-to-ground role, while JbG 35 (re-commissioned as JG 73 in 1995) and JbG 36 (re-commissioned as JG 72 in 1991) reversed these roles. Late in 1988, as German reunification began, all secondary roles were given up.

Technical development

The German Department of Defence initially intended to buy the Phantom to fill the gap until the Tornado – at that time still intended to be multi-role – could be introduced. German interest was focused on a simplified single seat version of the F-4E, though it soon became obvious that the reconstruction and evaluation costs would have vastly exceeded the budgeted DM4 billion. Consequently, a slightly modified F-4E was ordered, which would incorporate the following changes:
- No seventh fuel cell, unlike the RF-4E
- Non-slotted stabilators
- Simplified APQ 120-V-5 radar set
- No provisions for AIM-7 Sparrow missiles
- Introduction of leading edge slats to improve manoeuvrability

Early in 1975, studies showed it would be necessary to enhance the F-4F's capabilities to deliver conventional weapons. German Phantoms were well able to employ the ammunition already in use with the Luftwaffe, though not the newly-developed smart weapons. Another important point was to enhance its capability to use the armaments carried by USAF F-4s, which at that time numbered approximately 500 US F-4s in Central Europe. A Memorandum of Agreement, known as the PEACE RHINE Programme, was subsequently signed between the German and US governments, and this included a combat improvement programme for all GAF F-4Fs. The main contractor for the German side was the then Messerschmitt – Bölkow-Blöhm (MBB) now DaimlerChrysler Aerospace. The programme's core was the installation of a freely programmable LRU 1 weapons computer, to which a signal conditioner converter unit (SCCU) was added to increase its input and output capability. The programme changed analogue data into digital information. Other vital modifications were:
- Radar beacon for the APQ 120 radar to drop bombs though clouds.
- Installation of a digital scan converter group for radar and optical picture on the scope.
- Addition of computerised automatic acquisition to improve air-to-air combat.

- Replacement of Aero 3B launch rails by LAU 7A/5 (FRG) rails to accept AIM-9L missiles.
- Change of the weapons delivery panel to employ AGM-65B Maverick missiles.
- Improving the cockpit, including a Maverick modified hand control stick.
- Improvement of the inner wing pylon to carry the LAU 118 AGM-65 Maverick missile launch rail for a single missile on each rail.
- Introduction of AIM-9L Sidewinder missiles.
- Exchange of AN/ALR 46 radar warning gear for the AN/ALR 68 RHAW, specially developed for GAF needs by Litton.
- Retrofit of inner wing pylons with two AN/ALE 40 chaff and flare dispensers on either side of the pylon.
- Replacement of the Royal Jet 600 US gallon (2,270 litre) centreline tank by the High Performance Centreline tank taken from the F-15, which can withstand more 'g's during air-to-air combat.
- The Sparrow bays were *not* rewired, nor were launchers installed.

The upgrade programme began in 1980 and ended in 1984 with JG 74 'Mölders' and additionally a new camouflage was introduced, replacing the obsolete Norm 72-splinter scheme. This is referred to as Norm 81A/B, a camouflage which makes the F-4F less

detectable in air-to-air combat. PEACE RHINE was carried out on all surviving F-4Fs, no differentiation being made between F-4Fs intended for the attack role and those originally destined for interceptor duty. F-4Fs are able to carry the same weapons: US Mk 82 bombs, French Matra retarded bombs or British BL 755 cluster bomb units. Even the AGM-65 Mavericks can be employed by all the aircraft, giving the German Phantoms a certain stand-off capability.

In the late 1970s, it was rumoured that the Warsaw Pact was developing a new aircraft generation, more agile and manoeuvrable than the F-4, F-15 or any other aircraft in NATO's inventory. To counter this threat, Germany, Italy, Spain and the UK jointly developed the European Fighter Aircraft (Eurofighter) and until it is introduced, the F-4 Phantom II will stay in front-line service with the Luftwaffe.

Although the PEACE RHINE programme gave the Luftwaffe F-4Fs additional capabilities, it became clear, even before its completion, that this was insufficient to keep the aircraft effective until the planned retirement date. With the introduction of the Eurofighter (EFA) postponed to the 2003, the German Department of Defence decided to keep the remaining F-4Fs in service until 2012.

Above: *Target-towing has been the responsibility of Tracor Flight Systems Incorporated F-100Fs since mid-1989. Air to Air gunnery practice usually takes place in North Sea Danger Areas, although until 1998 such work had also been carried out at Deci.* ERIC KATERBERG

Below: *A German Air Force F-4F 72-1131 (formerly 37+21), wearing Norm 81B camouflage marks, of the 20th FS taxies in at Holloman AFB, New Mexico. Newly-qualified pilots spend 12 months there honing their fighter skills before returning to Europe — and that European weather!* AUTHOR

JG 71 based at Wittmundhaven painted this F-4F in special marks to celebrate 25 years of flying the type. It is seen here taxiing past the control tower at Norvenich. HERIBERT MENNEN

To ensure their safe and efficient operation beyond 2000, a three-stage improved combat efficiency (ICE) programme was begun in 1990 and ended in 1997. Two stages were intended for all the surviving 156 aircraft, the third and most important stage was destined for only 113 aircraft.

The first stage comprised a complete structural life extension programme (SLEP), which included:
• Lengthening the structural life for another 6,000 flight hours, with a potential life of about 10,000 flying hours.
• Extension of planned depot maintenance (PDM) intervals from 54 to 72 months, reducing the life-cycle cost significantly.
• Preventive inspections and repairs at an early date.
• Dividing the F-4 fuselage into structural inspection zones.

• Reworking areas found to have structural material fatigue.
• Introduction of the Norm 90J air superiority grey camouflage scheme in three different greys.

The SLEP was conducted during the PDM intervals. Smaller problems were solved immediately, though for larger problems, new parts were produced using the most modern production standards, and tools especially reworked for the task. Older parts, the logistical availability of which could no longer be ensured, were exchanged.

The second stage began in 1990 and comprised:
• Integration of a Honeywell Laser INS.
• A GEC Marconi digital air data computer CPU-143/A.
• A Rockwell-Collins control unit for the LINS.
• Installing a MIL STD 1553 digital databus.

The 43 F-4Fs which received only the first two stages of the ICE (or KWS - Kampfwertsteigerung in German) are referred to as ICE air-to-ground (KWS - Luftangriffsvarianten) variants, or more usually known as 'black noses' as they kept their black radomes.

The remaining 113 F-4Fs are known as ICE air defence variants (KWS - Luftverteidigungsvarianten) or 'grey noses' because of their grey radomes.

The third stage contains:
• Hughes AN/APG-65GY radar set, produced under licence by DASA Ulm.
• A Litef mission computer to increase the weapons computer's capacity.
• A new radar hand control panel for the rear cockpit.
• AIM-120 AMRAAM launch rails installed into the AIM-7 missile bays, provided by Airscrew Howden.
• A new grey radome by Marion Composites, optimised for the APG-65's emissions.

A total of 65 of these aircraft were upgraded at the DASA plant at Manching, Bavaria, and the remaining 48 F-4Fs at Luftwaffen Werft 62 (Luftwaffe maintenance facility) at Jever, in Northern Germany. The last ICE Phantom was rolled out in January 1997 at Jever. As the 2003 introduction date for the Eurofighter draws closer, no more money is being spent on further upgrades to the F-4F. A final attempt was made to improve the F-4F by introducing a new VHF/UHF radio, a VCR for radar, voice and HUD symbology recording, and a new IFF transponder. This kit is already in evaluation with JG 74'M', installed in 37+77 (72-1287). Whether it will be bought for all the remaining 150 Luftwaffe F-4s is not yet known: a decision is due in mid-2000, and if it goes ahead, it will be the final upgrade for the F-4 in GAF service.

Until the Eurofighter flies in German skies, the F-4F will remain as the front line fighter for the GAF. Wings due to be equipped with the new aircraft include: 71 'Richthofen' stationed at Wittmundhafen, Friesland, with about 30 F-4F

F-4F LOSSES

Date	GAF code	Serial	Site	Unit	Crew
22.04.75	37+68	72-1178	Stoffelhansenschwaig	JG 74	2 K
02.10.75	38+19	72-1229	2onm NW of Helgoland	JG 71	2 OK
16.05.76	37+59	72-1169	at Brockum/Diepholz	JG 71	2 Inj
06.06.77	37+87	72-1197	at Gross-Roscharden	JG 71	2 Inj
18.06.79	38+71	72-1281	into farm house near Detmold	JG 71	2 K
13.09.79	38+23	72-1233	into the sea 5nm NW Amrum	JG 71	1 K, 1 Inj
20.12.79	37+74	72-1184	crash at Mörzheim/Palatinate	FBW 35	2 K
22.09.80	38+65	72-1275	into lake 49nm NW Goose Bay	FBW 36	2 K
21.04.81	37+02	72-1112	at Remels	JG 71	2 K
18.07.81	38+22	72-1232	15nm E Goose Bay	JG 71	2 K
08.02.82	38+55	72-1245	ACMI Deci	JG 74	1 Inj, 1 K
03.05.82	37+62	72-1172	at the mouth of River Stör	FBW 36	2 K
06.12.83	38+41	72-1251	at Kettenkamp/Nortrup	FBW 36	1 Inj, 1 OK
31.01.85	37+95	72-1205	mid-air collision with 37+99	JG 71	1 K, 1 Inj
31.01.85	37+99	72-1209	mid-air collision with 37+95	JG 71	2 Inj
11.04.85	38+52	72-1262	into Bordeaux Harbour	JG 74	2 K
16.07.85	37+80	72-1190	at Tegernbach/Rudelzhausen	JG 74	2 K
24.03.87	37+27	72-1137	mid-air collision with 38+15	JG 71	2 K
24.03.87	38+15	72-1225	mid-air collision with 37+27	JG 71	2 Inj
22.04.93	37+51	72-1161	crash during airshow training	JG 72	2 K
22.09.94	37+46	72-1156	w/o after left engine on fire	FBW 35	2 OK
13.09.95	37+56	72-1166	crash at Haselbach after Vertigo	JG 74	2 K
24.04.96	38+59	72-1269	fire in cockpit, into North Sea	JG 72	2 Inj
04.06.98	37+73	72-1183	crash NW Goose Bay	JG 71	1 Inj, 1 K
14.10.98	38+72	72-1282	mid-air collision 38+21/72-1231	2oth FS	2 OK

Key: KIA- Killed In Action; Inj — Injured

ICE A/D variants; JG 72 'Westfalen' stationed at Rheine-Hopsten, Westfalia, equipped with 16 of either the F-4F ICE A/D and the A/G variant: JG 73 'Steinhoff' stationed at Laage, Mecklemburg, in a unique role as 23 MiG-29G aircraft are serving with the first squadron and 16 F-4F ICE A/D in the second; JG 74 'Mölders' stationed at Neuburg an der Donau, Bavaria, equipped with about 30 F-4F ICE A/D variants, and 20 FS at Holloman AB, New Mexico, with 16 F-4F ICE A/G and eight A/D variants for pilot training.

JG 73 will be the first wing to hand in its aircraft in 2003, followed by JG 74 in 2005. Up to now it is not clear whether the A/G aircraft will be replaced first, or together with the A/D variants.

Crew Training

The Luftwaffe does not have its own flight school in Germany, but is a partner in the Euro-NATO Joint Jet Pilot Training (EN-JJPT) scheme at Sheppard AFB, Texas, USA, where its combat pilots and weapons system officers are trained. At the 80th Training Wing, trainee pilots undergo the USAF training syllabus, flying a total of 132 hours on the Cessna T-37B before converting to the Northrop T-38 Talon for another 130 hours. Weapons system officers are qualified on the T-37B for basic familiarisation. Navigational training is conducted in Boeing T-43A (military B737) aircraft. As well as spending 85 hours on this aircraft, the WSOs undergo a large amount of time in simulator training over 15 months at NAS Pensacola, Florida.

Having proved their skills as pilots or WSOs, the newly 'winged' officers move on to Holloman AFB, New Mexico, where about 12 pilots are trained with the 20th FS each year. On their return to Germany, the non-combat-ready (NCR) F-4 pilots are sent to 2 Squadron of JG 72 for another three months. Having become used to the beautiful weather conditions in the US, they have to adjust to the bad weather and crowded skies of Europe, flying formations, 1 v 1 combat missions and tactical training. After this 'Europeanisation',

A JbG 35 F-4F prepares to depart Pferdsfeld in 1979. Note those very large numbers! VIA AUTHOR

the pilots return to their designated units and start the training that will take them, after about two years, to combat-ready status.

The respective wings divide their daily duties into three to four flying periods, enabling both squadrons to take part in the planned training by flying alternately in the first or second half of the working day. This system gives the pilot an average of 170-190 flight hours per year.

Goose Bay

Since 1980, the Luftwaffe has deployed annually to Goose Bay, Canada, for very low-level flying training. A German-Canadian agreement allows Luftwaffe pilots to fly at tree-top level above the Canadian wilderness. In Germany, this kind of flying is not permitted: strict safety regulations, densely populated areas and noise abatement procedures limit all missions to flights above 1,000ft (304m) from ground level. Crews due to deploy to Goose Bay begin training with air-to-air refuelling above Germany. The 2,600nm (4,800km) distance between the home base and Goose Bay has to be covered non-stop, making at least five tanker link-ups necessary. The first tanker is met by the F-4s above Scotland: the USAF provides KC-135 or KC-10 tankers stationed at Mildenhall. After giving the complete fuel load to the Phantoms, the tanker returns home. The Goose Bay detachment then links up with a second tanker coming from

the US, which waits for them on their route, somewhere in between Newfoundland and the British Isles. Training starts on the following day familiarising the pilots with the new altitudes and airspeeds. About five missions have to be conducted, starting at altitudes of 500ft (152m) down to 250ft (76m). The airspeed must not exceed 380 to 600kts (704 to 1,100km/h). The last two are flown at and below 100ft (30m). Once they are accustomed to the new environment, the German pilots fly intercept and combat missions under simulated war conditions; the threat being provided mainly by Dutch, Belgian or Canadian aircraft. To keep the exercise economic, eight or ten F-4Fs are taken from the Luftwaffe's operational wings and deployed to Canada at the beginning of the low-flying season, staying until the last fighter Wing has finished its training.

Decimomannu

Air-to-air combat and dog-fights have to take place in temporarily reserved air spaces in order to keep military aircraft well away from the dense civil air traffic routed around those areas. Due to the limited airspace available for Beyond Visual Range (BVR) engagements, and because of stringent safety regulations, the training of the fighter wings has become more and more of a problem, and to counter this, Luftwaffe fighter units deploy annually to Decimomannu on Sardinia. Over a six- to eight-week period, fighter pilots can train in the Air Combat and Manoeuvring Instrumentation (ACMI), unrestricted by noise abatement or any other regulations similar to those crippling them in Germany. The ACMI is located east of the island of Sardinia, over the sea, and is about 100nm (185km) long and 50nm (93km) wide. Even large-force employment scenarios, with more than 30 aircraft participating, can be carried out.

Until 1989, air-to-air gunnery against towed targets was conducted above the North Sea and the Mediterranean. Target-tow duties were undertaken by F-4F tug aircraft equipped with a modified A/A37 U-15 or a DATS-3 tow target system. The vast amount of flight hours needed and the decreasing serviceability of the F-4F, however, led to a decision in mid-1989 to have the tug duties flown by a civil contracted F-100 from Tracor Flight Systems Incorporated. These F-100s are stationed at Wittmundhaven and work closely with JG 71 'R'. However, in 1998, the Italian authorities decided that civil-owned aircraft should no longer be allowed to use military bases, thus bringing to an end ten years of safe air-to-air gunnery above Sardinia. Today

Showing off its teeth! An F-4F of JG 72 gives the camera a close-up. AUTHOR

A WSO waves to the camera as he and the pilot of a JG 71 F-4F taxi out to the threshold at Nellis AFB, in October 1996. AFM-ALAN WARNES

the Luftwaffe relies exclusively on conducting these operations in Danger Areas over the North Sea. At least once during their service, F-4F pilots are given the opportunity to fire a live AIM-9 missile on a flare target towed by a Learjet 35 of Gesellschaft für Flugzieldarstellung (GFD), stationed at Hohn AB.

RED FLAG

A milestone for the Phantom aircrew is taking part in a major exercise such as RED FLAG, held at Nellis AFB, Nevada, or MAPLE FLAG, at Cold Lake, Canada. In 1996, German F-4s took part in RED FLAG for the first time, and now will participate every two years.

The first wing to deploy to Nellis was JG 71 'Richthofen' in September 1996, after finishing low-level training at Goose Bay. Eight F-4Fs brought to Nellis provided Defensive Counter Air (DCA) and Offensive Counter Air (OCA) assets. As DCA they used real wartime BVR employment procedures for the first time. Performing OCA, F-4s simulated MiG-29s and Su-27s for the F-15, F-16, F-117 and Tornado F.3 crews taking part. In October 1996, JG 71 was relieved by JG 72 for a four-week period. The third and last fighter wing to take part in RED FLAG 1997 was JG 74 from Neuburg, which redeployed by the end of November 1997.

JG 73's turn to take part in RED FLAG came in September 1999. Following a three-week exercise in Goose Bay, six F-4Fs and six MiG-29s arrived at Nellis on November 3. The MiG-29s, fitted with additional under-wing tanks, conducted aggressor duties together with Nellis-based F-16Cs. Due to their lack of long-range capability, and missing in-flight refuelling provisions, the MiGs had to stop over at Tonopah airfield after each mission they flew. The F-4s provided Blue Air assets, flying directly from Nellis and being refuelled in the air by a KC 135 tanker. Average mission duration for the F-4F pilots was nearly two hours, with four missions a day. An F-4 pilot said: " RED FLAG is the most demanding exercise I ever took part in. There are so many aircraft in the air and a lot of restrictions have to be taken into consideration. The complexity of the missions flown brings you to the limits of your physical and psychological abilities. Mistakes are easily made, even in an F-4F with a second crewman aboard to halve the workload. Too many lives are in danger if you screw up". F-4 crews will continue to take part in these highly valuable exercises until 2012 when their aircraft are finally retired.

F-4 tactics

Air-to-air combat tactics are based mainly on the weapons system's abilities. During the first decades of the F-4F's service life, it lacked the ability to employ BVR weapons, such as the American AIM-7 Sparrow missile or the British Skyflash. Even the IR AIM-9B missile promised no advantage against the anticipated Warsaw Pact enemy because it had to be fired at the enemy's heat exhaust. On the other hand, even shot from the best position, these missiles were quite unreliable, as the Vietnam War proved to US aircrews.

Three standard duties are performed by German F-4Fs:
• Combat Air Patrol (CAP), guarding a particular airspace and preventing the enemy from breaking through.
• Sweep, flying well in front of a bomber package, fighting their way though enemy CAPs and air defence installations.
• Escort, protecting friendly bombers and valuable air assets by staying close to them.
Because of their age and the downgrading of the F-4F air frame, Luftwaffe F-4s have certain disadvantages:
• Smoking J79-GE-17A engines, rendering it rather visible in the sky. A modification kit was thought to be too costly, considering its anticipated short service time.
• Down-graded APQ120 radar: several features of the F-4E radar were not included.
• No BVR capability: the AIM-7 launchers were not provided.
• No IFF interrogator, which means the crew have to rely on visual or other means of identification.
• Lack of agility: it was introduced to match the MiG-21 but not modern third generation aircraft.

These problems led to tactics which included heavy manoeuvring and rapid altitude changes, making it difficult for enemy aircraft to track or see the Phantom. The aim of these tactics is for one F-4 to reach the enemy's 'six o'clock' position undetected, while the chased second F-4 is – hopefully – still outside his weapons envelope.

This kind of tactic was retained until the early 1990s, when the ICE upgrade showed its efficiency. With the introduction of the new APG-65 radar set and the AIM-120 AMRAAM missile, still believed to be the best air-to-air combat equipment combination, the tactics rapidly changed from short-range visual engagements to long-range engagements covering a distance of 30-40nm (55-74km). Unfortunately, there are still many disadvantages with today's F-4s, though Phantom crews are now in a position to stay out of the enemy's reach while at the same time they are able to destroy him from a distance. Descriptive words such as 'wall formation' or 'grinder', said to be the best tactics in which to employ BVR missiles, were for a long time the privilege of F-15 or FGR.2 pilots. Now they are in the vocabulary of every German fighter pilot. Of course, well-executed manoeuvres can defeat a BVR shot, and a Phantom crew can easily find itself fighting the enemy visually. So, the older tactics were not just given up, but enhanced and are now a vital part of BVR employment. F-4

A German Phantom moves up for fuel from an American KC-135 tanker. The Germans do not have their own tanker aircraft and therefore generally use US assistance to venture to such places as Goose Bay, Canada. AFM-DUNCAN CUBITT

Phantom upgrades

Michael J Gething looks at upgrades that have been carried out on current Phantom fleets.

THE MCDONNELL Douglas F-4 Phantom II continues to serve many useful roles within nine air forces around the world. Most of these countries have either carried out a capability or mid-life upgrade on their aircraft or are planning one. This is the state-of-play at the turn of the century.

Egypt

The first Egyptian F-4s were delivered in 1979 and 32 still serve in the air defence and attack roles. To date, only periodic structural and safety modifications have been made. Although plans to upgrade these Phantoms have been studied, there is not thought to be a firm programme in place.

Germany

Some 151 German F-4F Phantoms remain in service. Between 1975 and 1983, the PEACE RHINE programme upgraded the APQ-120 radar, introduced the AIM-9L Sidewinder air-to-air missile (AAM), made provision for the AGM-65 Maverick air-to-ground missile and added software enhancements. In 1983, Germany initiated the Improved Combat Efficiency (ICE) programme for 110 of its F-4Fs. The Military Aircraft Division of MBB (now DaimlerChrysler Aerospace - DASA) was contracted for the ICE programme, which began in December 1986. A further 40 F-4Fs, serving in the fighter-bomber role, have undergone a partial update (databus, INS and air data computer).

The core of the ICE programme was the replacement of the existing radar with a licence-built Hughes (now Raytheon) APG-65 multi-mode radar and provision for four AIM-120 advanced medium air-to-air missiles (AMRAAMs). Also included were a TST radar control console, revised cockpit displays, Litef computer, Honeywell H-423 ring-laser gyro inertial navigation system (INS), Marconi Avionics CPU-143/A digital air data computer, new Identification Friend or Foe, Frazer-Nash AMRAAM launchers, a MIL-STD-1553B databus with advanced software, and improved electronic countermeasures (ECM) resistance.

The first F-4F ICE flew on May 2, 1990, and AIM-120 AMRAAM firing trials took place from October 1991 to September 1992. Fleet conversion began in July 1991, with deliveries from April 1992. The ICE programme was completed in October 1996 (for more details, see *German Evolution*, page 56).

Greece

See *Aegean Upgrades*, page 38.

Iran

Deliveries of Phantoms to the former Imperial Iranian Air Force began with the F-4D in 1968, followed by the 'E models in 1971. Cut off from support structures since the revolution in 1979, the numbers have dwindled to approximately 40 F-4D/Es and six RF-4Es. There have been no known upgrades of these aircraft, although safety modifications are known to have been made and some locally-instigated weapons developments carried out.

Israel

Some 95 examples of the F-4E known as Kurnass (English translation: Sledgehammer) remain in Israeli service, with ten RF-4Es (Orefs – Ravens). In addition, two of the three F-4E (Special) reconnaissance aircraft remain, modified by General Dynamics (now Lockheed Martin Tactical Aircraft Systems) to carry a LOROP (long-range, oblique optical) camera system.

By the mid-1980s, Israel was looking to extend the life of its F-4E Phantom fleet beyond 2000. Two programmes were initiated by Israel Aircraft Industries (IAI): one to re-engine the fleet with the Pratt & Whitney PW1120 turbojet (20,620lb st [91.7kN], with afterburning) in place of the original J79; the other to offer an avionics/structural upgrade.

The Super Phantom re-engining programme began as a test-bed programme for the PW1120s selected for the indigenous Lavi fighter. The prototype first flew on April 24, 1987, and flight test results indicated significant performance improvements over the J79-powered F-4. Hopes for a full IAF retrofit programme ended with the cancellation of the Lavi. The Phantom 2000 (or Kurnass 2000) structural/avionics upgrade programme involved reinforced skins and fuel cells in fuselage and wings; complete rewiring; a dual MIL-STD-1553B databus; replaced and re-routed hydraulic lines; a reduction of avionics boxes; built-in test equipment; small strakes above the air intake flanks; and a revised cockpit layout.

The core of the new avionics system, integrated by Elbit Systems, is a derivative of Elbit's ACE-3 computer and the Norden (now Northrop Grumman) APG-76 multi-mode radar. Also included were an El-Op (Kaiser licence) wide-angle head-up display (HUD) with diffractive-optics, Elbit multi-function displays for both crew members, hands-on throttle and stick (HOTAS) controls, integrated comms and comms/nav system, improved ECM and self-protection systems.

The first redeliveries of the Phantom 2000 began in April 1989 and first operational use followed on February 5, 1991. The programme was completed in late 1994.

Japan

As the last of the 140 F-4EJs built by Mitsubishi Heavy Industries were delivered on May 20, 1981, a major equipment and weapon system update for the Japanese Air Self-Defence Force (JASDF) F-4EJ fleet was initiated.

A new Westinghouse (now part of Northrop Grumman) J/APG-66J radar was installed, with look-down/shoot-down capability, using AIM-7E/F Sparrow or AIM-9P/L Sidewinder AAMs. Other new sub-systems included the

Above: *IAI used Kurnass 334 as a test-bed for the Lavi's Pratt & Whitney PW1120 engine. First flight with one PW1120 and one General Electric J79 was on July 31, 1986, while first flight with two PW1120s followed on April 27, 1987. The aircraft was displayed at the 1987 Paris Air Show as Super Phantom 4X-JPA/229. The demise of the Lavi also killed the Super Phantom programme.* SHLOMO ALONI

Left: *The most common weapon used by the Kurnass 2000 in recent years during operations over Lebanon is the Laser Guided Bomb (LGB). Two variations are carried here by Kurnass 2000 659.*
SHLOMO ALONI

Litton J/ASN-4 INS, HUD, and J/APR-4Kai radar warning receiver. As well as new Mitsubishi AAM-3 missiles, the upgraded F-4EJ can carry two ASM-1C anti-shipping missiles. The AIM-120 AMRAAM may be adopted before the aircraft are retired.

Designated F-4EJ-Kai, the prototype first flew on July 17, 1984, and was re-delivered to the JASDF on December 13, 1984. Plans to convert 100 of JASDF's 125 remaining F-4EJs to F-4EJ-Kai configuration were reduced by attrition to 90 aircraft. The programme is now complete. The JASDF's 14 RF-4E reconnaissance Phantoms have also been upgraded, receiving the Texas Instruments (now Raytheon) APQ-172 forward-looking radars and a Melco-developed variant of the Thomson-CSF Astac electronic intelligence (ELINT) pod. In addition, 17 F-4EJs have been converted to RF-4EJ configuration.

The original F-4EJ cockpit (above) has been radically upgraded by Mitsubishi Heavy Industries as can be seen here (right). YOSHITOMO AOKI

South Korea

The first F-4D Phantoms were ex-USAF examples transferred to the Republic of Korea in August 1969, and 60 remain. These were followed by 104 new-build F-4Es from September 1977, of which 55 remain. South Korea received RF-4C 'Photo-Phantoms' in December 1990, and 18 are still extant.

The South Koreans have been endeavouring to upgrade some of their F-4Es for several years and Rockwell's North American Aircraft Modification Division (now part of Boeing) was actually selected for the task, but the contract was never signed. There is still potential for an upgrade.

Spain

The first Spanish RF-4Cs (Spanish designation CR.12) entered service in October 1978. Further aircraft arrived in January 1989 and 14 'Photo-Phantoms' remain in service. These aircraft feature the fixed, external in-flight refuelling probe, originally introduced on Israeli Phantoms. It is unlikely these aircraft will now be upgraded.

Turkey

See *Aegean Upgrades*, page 39.

Phantoms in Vietnam

Warren E Thompson looks at the role the Phantom during the Vietnam War.

S INCE THE DAYS of World War One, when the aeroplane came into its own as a weapon of war, only a handful of fighter types became legends during their brief tours of duty. During World War Two, there were numerous thoroughbred fighters such as the Mustang, Corsair and Lightning. A few short years later, in the Korean War, it was the F-86 Sabre and MiG-15 that captured the public's imagination. By the time that the Vietnam War had escalated far enough to merit close coverage by the media, it was the big, powerful F-105 and F-4 that dominated the dangerous missions into Route Pack VI over Hanoi. They were to be the primary strike aircraft that ran the gauntlet, daily, over North Vietnam carrying the war to the heart of the enemy.

The F-86, during its day, never had the versatility of the F-4, nor did the F-105. The fighters that were produced in this new era of sophisticated Triple-A and SAM missiles, had to be capable of mastering multiple roles. During the very early stages of Vietnam, it was the

older B-26, T-28, AC-47, B-57 and F-102 that assumed the tasking. As the war heated up and the MiG-17s began to appear, the F-4 Phantom made its first appearance in 1964.

Killing MiGs

Numerically, the most significant build-up of F-4s took place during 1965. This time-frame saw all three branches (USAF, Marines and Navy) depend heavily on this aircraft to handle a wide range of assignments. This increase was well covered by the Press, and Hanoi reacted with a significant increase in its MiG-17 inventory and delivery of a large number of the new MiG-21s. In anticipation of what was to come, Hanoi also bolstered its air-defences in the Hanoi/Haiphong area. The military leaders knew that it was just a matter of time before the Americans would begin bringing their F-4s over key targets and in the long term, it would be the SAMs that posed a bigger threat to the Phantoms than did the speedy little MiG-21s.

Up until this time, the Navy had the premier air superiority fighter in the F-8 Crusader. It was rapidly being replaced within the Fleet. During the 1965 period, the Navy's Phantoms and Crusaders were on the carriers in equal numbers, so both were still very much involved in the day-to-day responsibilities. The competitiveness between each of these pilot types has proven to be legendary in Navy folklore. Moving into the autumn of 1965, the primary USAF Phantom bases were all located in Thailand, while the Marines would be limited to DaNang. The Navy had F-4s out on both 'Yankee' and 'Dixie' Stations off the coast of North and South Vietnam.

The first 'official' front line squadron to operate in theatre was the famous 'Triple Nickel' outfit (555th TFS) that deployed from its home base at George AFB, California over to Thailand (Ubon) with a brief stop-over at Naha AB Okinawa. Beginning on April 23, 1966, the squadron would become one of the dominating MiG killer outfits operating the F-4. Over the next 12 months, it accounted for 12 confirmed kills. These were spread out over both the MiG-17s and MiG-21s.

It did not take long for the North Vietnamese to become proficient in Soviet intercept tactics. They used their ground controllers to perfection

Above: *A flight of 390th Tactical Fighter Squadron Phantoms soak up fuel from a KC-135 while en route to targets over Route Pack VI. This was taken in February 1970. At the time, the squadron was part of the elite 366th Wing, known as the 'Gun Fighters'. Note that the primary ordnance load consists of daisy cutters.* KEN SMITH

Below: *The USS Constellation (CVA-64) prepares to launch another of its Phantoms off the coast of Vietnam in August 1966. This F-4 was assigned to the VF-151 'Vigilantes'. They were deployed to the waters off North Vietnam on seven different occasions. Their home port during these combat tours was Atsugi, Japan.* JOE SZABO

The Marine 'Bengals' of VMFA-542 was one of the first units to take the Phantom into the hostile environment of Vietnam, shown here at DaNang in December 1965. The unit had moved from Japan over to DaNang in the early summer of 1965. This was the same squadron that flew its Grumman F7F-3N Tigercats over North Korea during the early months of the Korean War. ED SHARROW

Right: *Pilots from the 390th Fighter Squadron gather around for a group picture in between missions. This outfit was part of the 366th Wing, known as the 'Gunfighters'. The squadron would gain world attention later on when it became the first operational EF-111 unit.* KEN SMITH

Below: *Captain William Swendner, who probably made the second MiG-21 kill for the Air Force, on July 14, 1966, poses in front of his Phantom right after the mission. Captain Swendner and his back-seater, 1st Lt Duane Buttell, were assigned to the 480th Squadron of the 35th Tactical Fighter Wing based at DaNang during 1966.* DUANE BUTTELL

and they knew exactly when and where to hit the incoming strike packages which were made up of the Navy's A-4 Skyhawks and the Air Force's F-105 Thuds. For most of the war, this orchestrated hit-and-run strategy worked well and it made intercepting the MiGs extremely difficult for the F-4s. It wasn't until August 10, 1967, that the Navy Phantoms got a chance to lock up with the MiG-21s at close quarters.

The USS *Constellation* (CVA-64) was on Yankee Station in the Gulf of Tonkin. VF-142's F-4Bs were riding shotgun on an ALPHA STRIKE package when a swarm of MiG-21s met the force. The Phantoms were ready as *Red Crown*, their radar intercept ship off the coast, had the bandits pinpointed. Lt Guy Freeborn and Lt Cmdr Bob Davis locked on and fired within seconds of the intercept. Freeborn recalls, "I got a lock on the first MiG and got off a Sidewinder. It hit him, but he didn't go down. His left wing was streaming fuel. Bob Davis also fired two Sparrows at my MiG's wingman and both of the missiles went stupid! I got another tone, but the missile misfired. At that instant, Davis fired two Sidewinders and they both hit a MiG-21 that I was locked on to. All of the MiGs were manoeuvering violently

during the fight and I switched to another '21 and got a good tone. My number 3 Sidewinder tracked perfectly and the enemy aircraft disintegrated from the explosion. Within seconds, both of us had scored the first MiG-21 kills for the Navy. It was a memorable day for all of us."

Many details of the early MiG skirmishes were sketchy because they happened so fast. The MiGs always struck swiftly and the F-4s retaliated the same way. Once a few missiles were fired, if there were survivors, they disappeared in a matter of seconds.

The year that brought the Phantoms and MiGs into the most violent encounters was 1967. North Vietnam realised that the war was escalating so fast that its country would soon be blasted by American bombs and none of its assets would be safe. That is why it pushed a large number of MiG-17s and MiG-21s against the growing F-4 and F-105 numbers. It would also prove to be one of the most successful for the Thud in the air-to-air arena.

By December 31, 1967, the Phantoms had confirmed MiG kills totalling 36.5, while the F-105s scored 22.5 kills. These were some impressive figures, but the North Vietnamese

Air Force was, by no means, weakened to the point of being incapable of resisting the large strike forces being sent north by the Air Force and Navy.

Without a doubt, the F-4 proved to be the most versatile fighter in US Air Force history during the late 1960s. During the course of the war, it would master the air superiority, close air support, interdiction, MiG CAP, air defence, long-range bombardment, night fighter and reconnaissance tasking. Also, in between Vietnam and DESERT STORM, it would excel in the Wild Weasel role. However, of all these assignments, it is remembered by most as the 'MiG killer'. The US Navy was the first of the services to realise the potential of the aircraft and it ordered large numbers that would make it the primary defender of the fleet, replacing the F-8 Crusader.

The US Marines were attracted early on to the Phantom and the reason was not for its air-to-air fighting ability. They wanted a heavy hauler that could slug it out with anything that got in its way. The first Marine squadron to arrive in Vietnam was VMFA-531 *Grey Ghosts* . It set up shop at DaNang AB with its full complement of 15 aircraft, in April 1965, and immediately began supporting its troops in-country. These aircraft had been requested by General Westmoreland because they could execute a duel role over both the South and North. Squadron commander, Lt Colonel McGraw led the first flight of four F-4Bs from Cubi Point, Philippines into DaNang after a five-hour flight. They refuelled en route, from two Marine KC-130s.

Killing equation

For most of the Vietnam war, the strike packages that penetrated deep into the 'No-Man's Land' of Route Pack VI, it was the F-105s carrying the iron and the F-4s flying cover and protecting the Thuds from the lightning fast attacks from the MiGs. All three of these aircraft types were like magnets in that they attracted each other; the F-105s drew up the MiGs, which in turn brought in the Phantoms etc. On July 14, 1966, the 480th TFS drew the short straw and sent its F-4Cs into harm's

PHANTOM KILL DATA (MiG-21)				
Crew	Sqn	Weapon	Date	Type
First USAF Phantom MiG-21 kill over Vietnam:				
Major Paul J Gilmore/1st Lt William T Smith	48oth TFS/ 35th TFW	AIM-9 Missile	April 26, 1966	Flying an F-4C
First US Navy Phantom MiG-21 kill over Vietnam:				
Lt Guy H Freeborn/Lt jg (Junior Grade) Robert J Elliot	VF-142/	AIM-9	August 10,	Flying an
Lt Cmdr Robert C Davis/Lt Cmdr Gayle O Elie	CVW-14	Missile	1967	F-4B
(Both scored kills seconds apart)				
Final USAF Phantom MiG-21 kill over Vietnam:				
Captain Paul D Howman/1st Lt Lawrence W Kullman	4th TFS/ 432nd TRW	AIM-7 Missile	January 8, 1973	Flying F-4D
Final US Navy Phantom MiG-21 kill over Vietnam:				
Ltjg Scott H Davis/ Ltjg Geoffrey H Ulrich	VF-142/ CVW-14	AIM-9 Missile	December 28, 1972	Flying F-4J
Note: A US Navy Phantom is credited with the first aerial kill of the war (a MiG-17):				
Ltjg Terence M Murphy/Ensign Ronald J Fegan	VF-96/ CVW-9	AIM-7 Missile	April 9, 1965	Flying F-4B

A 'Night Owl' Phantom hooks up with its tanker in the late afternoon. The 497th Squadron was tasked with protecting the gunships that were flying to the North after dark. Usually one of its F-4s stayed in the area while the other was on the tanker. This type of mission could last for several hours.
NOLAN SCHMIDT

One of the most specialised squadrons to fly the Phantom was the 497th Tactical Fighter Squadron's 'Night Owls'. It was the only dedicated night fighter unit to operate the F-4 during the Vietnam War. Its crews had to undergo 15 checkout rides before they were certified to fly the night attack mission. They formed part of the famed 8th Wing. RAY MARZULLO

Sunset over the Gulf of Tonkin. This F-4C from an unidentified squadron hits the tanker before returning to its base in South Vietnam. This was taken in December 1965, before the Phantoms took on their camouflage paint scheme. LUCKY EKMAN

'All of the MiGs were manoeuvering violently during the fight and I switched to another '21 and got a good tone. My number 3 Sidewinder tracked perfectly and the enemy aircraft disintegrated from the explosion. Within seconds, both of us had scored the first MiG-21 kills for the Navy.'

way. Minutes after the MiG-21s struck, the 480th would chalk up two confirmed kills at the hands of the AIM-9 missiles. Its F-4Cs could carry a very lethal load into an aerial duel, that was capable of handling any aircraft type that North Vietnam could put up against them. These weapons consisted of four Sparrows and four Sidewinders. If they were also tasked with close air support, they could hang eight Mk 83 bombs on the pylons. Neither model of MiG fighters, in theatre, could come close to this payload. The weapon-of-choice for the Phantom was the AIM-9 Sidewinder which accounted for more kills than any other weapon type, in Vietnam.

One of the scoring pilots, Captain William Swendner, recalls the furious action; "On this day, we were escorting some F-105 Wild Weasels over the Black River, inbound for Hanoi. One of the Thuds had aborted, so we were four Phantoms protecting three '105s. We were at about 10,000 feet when the Thuds called a right turn to set up for a Shrike release against a SAM site that had just lit up. As we made the turn, my #3 called out a MiG at 8 o'clock.

I reversed my turn to the left, jettisoned external tanks and the MiG-21 blew through the formation at a very high rate of speed, disappearing into the haze. At that time, we picked up the Thuds again and spotted another '21 coming in behind the #3 Weasel. I called out for him to break right and I pointed the nose of my F-4 straight at the intruder. It was hard to get a lock-on because we were pointed at the ground and picking up a lot of ground clutter.

I fired a missile from in close and it didn't have time to arm. I kept trying to slow my aircraft down as I was almost underneath the MiG. At that moment, I saw him light his afterburner and break-up to the right. That is when I knew I had him. I let him accelerate out about 1,500 feet and pulled in behind him. The next shot was with a Sidewinder and malfunctioned and blew up about 800 feet out.

"I tracked him again and had a good growl in the headset from his tailpipe heat, so I fired a third Sidewinder. The missile appeared to go out of sight and I figured it had missed, when all of a sudden the MiG-21 disintegrated in front of me. The missile must have gone up into his tailpipe before blowing. I pulled to the left to avoid the debris, the biggest piece of which was a wing.

There was no parachute. All of this action occurred about 25 miles northwest of Hanoi. Another of our Phantoms scored a kill in the same fight. It had been a great day for hunting, as the Weasels destroyed the SAM site

All of the aircrews assigned to the 'Triple Nickel' Squadron take the time to pose for a group picture outside of their Operation Building at Ubon. WALTER RADEKER

and we bagged two MiG-21s."

Night operations and recce

One of the most significant roles that was perfected by the F-4 during the war was that of the night fighter/attack. One squadron, the 497th TFS, was given this difficult assignment and they became known as the 'Night Owls'. Developing the skills required to carry this out proved time-consuming to say the least. The aircrews had to have a 15-ride checkout before being allowed to assume normal rotation within the squadron. The 497th Phantoms had very few external lights showing and the cockpit lights were almost too dim to read the instruments. The requests for their services almost exceeded the equipment that was available. They participated in flare dispensing, Loran bombing, AC-130 gunship escort and multiple aerial refuellings... all at night. Some of their most difficult jobs were involved as AC-130 escorts, which drew an enormous amount of ground fire. With each AC-130, there were usually three F-4s. They would work relays back and forth to the tankers and over the target area. This was necessary because the '130s could spend hours over a specific target area, so their legs were much longer than that of the F-4.

The missiles that were used by the Phantoms were proven killers though slightly erratic. In cases where the F-4 and MiGs locked up at close range, these weapons were useless. If they didn't have time to arm, they would simply pass up the target and detonate in the distance. A large number of pilots stated that there was a definite need for these multi-purpose fighters to be fitted with guns. In May 1967, some of the F-4s were fitted with gun

'That is when I knew I had him. I let him accelerate out about 1,500 feet and pulled in behind him. The next shot was with a Sidewinder and malfunctioned and blew up about 800 feet out.'

pods which contained a 20mm Gatling gun.

On May 14, the 489th TFS found itself in a fight with a swarm of MiG-17s. When it was over, the Phantoms had claimed three enemy aircraft, two of which were downed by the guns. The parent Wing was the 366th which quickly became known as the 'Gunfighters'.

High-speed reconnaissance over Route Pack VI became essential in planning out targets to hit. Once the RF-101 had exited the theatre, it was up to the RF-4Cs of the Air Force and the big RA-5C Vigilantes from the Navy to provide this intelligence. The North Vietnamese went after these camera ships with everything they could

throw at them. Due to the heavy MiG activity in these areas, they always had Phantom escorts with them. The RF-4C made its initial appearance in SEA on October 30, 1965, when the 16th Tactical Reconnaissance Squadron deployed over from Shaw AFB. It settled in at Ton Son Nhut and was assigned to operate under control of the 460th TRWg. The Marine's VMCJ-1 brought in its RF-4Bs to DaNang AB and pulled heavy tasking, in-country.

F-4s with everything

The presence of the F-4 in the Vietnam War impacted the operational status of more front

Left: *100 Mission patch for the RF-4C. These were worn by aircrew members who had accomplished the required number of unarmed missions over hostile territory.*
Below: *The Phantoms proved to be one of the most versatile combat aircraft ever to be operated by the USAF. Not only could they fight the MiGs on the vertical, but they could accurately deliver just about any type of ordnance in the inventory. These ordnance carts show a selection of what they carried.* MILAN ZIMER

line aircraft types than had occurred since World War Two. This time, the United States was only involved in a very unpopular regional war. During the early years of the conflict, the US Navy depended on the A-4 Skyhawk to carry the bombs and the F-8 Crusader to guarantee air superiority.

The Phantom came along and phased both of them out. The Marine Corps depended on both of these types to support its troops until they brought in the F-4 to carry the iron. From the USAF side of it, they depended on the F-102 to provide air defence of its key bases – the RF-101 Voodoo to make the camera sweeps over the north and the F-100 Super Sabre to carry

the bombs. All three of these credible types were replaced by the F-4. This trend continued on to present day where the number of aircraft types have dwindled down to a select few, and it was the Phantom that eliminated the era of specialised military attack aircraft.

The multi-purpose Phantom put unusually heavy pressure on its air crews and maintenance personnel. Not only did it excel in the long war fought in Vietnam, it was a major player within the ranks of the Air National Guard and Air Force Reserves throughout the 1970s and 1980s.

It was still in front line service when DESERT SHIELD/STORM began in late 1990, seeing serious

action in the role of Wild Weasel and Photo Reconnaissance. It is easy to look back and figure out where things went wrong and what might have been.... However, the F-4's kill ratio would have been significantly higher, had the military leadership been able to dictate the terms of the war. There were just too many restrictions put on American air power to deliver the war to a successful conclusion. The fact that all the branches of the American military used the Phantom in large numbers, only served as a catalyst for other countries to follow suit. There were over 5,000 Phantoms built and they have served the military in at least 20 countries.

Above: *WSO 1st Lt Milan Zimer points to the three confirmed kills that he was credited with while flying the F-4C with the 389th Fighter Squadron. All three were MiG-21s that were bagged between May 20-22, 1967.* MILAN ZIMER

Left: *The blue trim and tail code – BT indicated that this F-4C was flown by the 390th TFS out of DaNang. Note the heavy load of ordnance ready to be delivered into Route Pack VI. Even though the F-4 was one of the fastest fighter bombers to do time over North Vietnam, the type was also effective in delivering napalm, which usually favoured the slower aircraft.* BRYAN ALEKSICH

Vietnam Ops

Above: *The Vietnam War saw the first large-scale use of air-to-air refuelling, a considerable number of KC-135A Stratotankers being used. A pair of 432nd TRW F-4Es await their turn to fill up alongside a pair of F-105 Thunderchiefs.*

Left: *The 555th TFS 'Triple Nickel' was one of the most famous units of the Vietnam War, where it was subordinate to the 432nd TRW. Today it lives on as part of the 31st FW at Aviano AB in Italy. Here a 'Triple Nickel' Phantom releases its load of bombs over a North Vietnamese target.*

Right *September 1972 at Takhli – an impressive array of F-4s provides visual confirmation of the scale of Phantom involvement in the Vietnam War.*

NATIONAL ARCHIVES

Left: *Dramatic view from the wing-man's rear cockpit as the flight leader commences his bombing run against a North Vietnamese target.*
ALL PHOTOS VIA PAUL CRICKMORE

Below: *Two early CBU dispenser units are clearly visible beneath the wings of F-4D 66-0262/'OC' of the 13th TFS/432nd TRW – note the single AIM-7 Sparrow air-to-air missile. The 432nd TRW operated from Udorn RTAFB in Thailand during the Vietnam War and was later redesignated the 432nd TFW on November 15, 1974.*

Below: *The 'Silver Eagles' of Marine Squadron VMFA-115 finished long tours in Vietnam while operating out of Nam Phong, Thailand. Having just taken off from its base, this Phantom is pulling back from the tanker ready for a mission over the North. The ordnance load consisted of Mk 82 GP bombs.*
ED EDELEN

Bottom: *F-4E 67-0385/'JJ' of the 34th TFS/388th TFW soars over Vietnam en route to its target – note the long proximity arming fuses fitted to the bombs. The unit operated from Korat RTAFB in Thailand during the conflict.*

Combat over Iraq

AFM's Iranian correspondent Farzin Nadimi examines the role of Iran's F-4 Phantoms in the war with Iraq.

The backseater of this F-4E Phantom is Lt Gen Abbas Babaie, an Iranian war hero and the then deputy-commander of IRIAF. After flying many daring combat missions he was reportedly killed by a direct AAA hit to the cockpit; however, the exact cause of his death is still shrouded in secrecy.

ALL PHOTOS VIA AUTHOR, UNLESS STATED

PRIOR TO THE Islamic Revolution, Iran was one of the largest overseas operators of the F-4 Phantom. A total of 177 F-4Es, 32 F-4Ds, and 16 RF-4Es (plus eight F-4Es borrowed from the USA and subsequently returned) were supplied to Iran before the fall of the Mohammad-Reza Shah. The rise of the Islamic Republic cut off further arms supplies, after a formal arms embargo was imposed on February 28, 1979. Consequently, the remaining 31 F-4Es and 16 or 11 (the exact figure is disputed) RF-4Es destined for Iran were never delivered. At this time, Iran had almost 188 operational Phantoms. Contrary to Western reports, F-4 squadrons managed to maintain their combat effectiveness despite widespread political upheavals and personnel purges. Technical malfunctions, often appearing during flight preparation, would reduce the flight packages, but missions were seldom aborted for this reason.

The outbreak of the Iraq-Iran War on the afternoon of September 22, 1980, resulted in the newly re-organised Islamic Republic of Iran Air Force (IRIAF) having to rely heavily on its F-4 Phantom units. This legendary veteran fighter-bomber was definitely the star of the IRIAF during the eight-year war with Iraq, performing virtually every combat role, from pure fighter to deep-penetration interdictor. Phantoms were to play a key role in most of the missions far into Iraqi territory, in many cases returning to base after sustaining heavy combat

of the runway, after the crew had already ejected. Later, the aircraft's wing was replaced, the first time such work had been undertaken in Iran, and it was returned to combat service.

The first months of the war saw the IRIAF making concentrated efforts to halt the Iraqi ground advance, often directly engaging tank and vehicle columns, sometimes at altitudes as low as 10-13 ft (3-4m). Iraqi MiG-21 and MiG-23 fighters were used as top cover to protect their military columns heading toward Iran, and as a result there were many air-to-air encounters – with mixed results.

Operation PEARL

The Iraqis had positioned radar and monitoring equipment on the Al-Bakr and Al-Omayeh oil rigs in the northern part of the Persian Gulf, because a large number of Iranian air operations were routed from near these installations. As a result, a combined air/sea operation, code-named morvarid (Pearl), was initiated by Iranian Navy Task Force 421 on November 28, 1980, to neutralise these two platforms.

An Iranian La Combattante II missile-equipped fast patrol craft, named Peykan, was engaging Iraqi surface vessels and aircraft, calling for air support when the situation got out of control. Two F-4Es, each carrying four AGM-65A Maverick missiles, were scrambled and flew at 400kts and 20-50ft (6-15m) above the sea, increasing speed and altitude to 500kts and 4,000ft (1,200m) once over the area. Seven Iraqi vessels were destroyed with

damage. The F-4's baptism of fire during the war with Iraq came as an unexpected one. The conflict began with an Iraqi air attack on six Iranian air bases and four Iranian army barracks, followed by a land offensive deep into the country at four points along a 435-mile (700km) front. This first Iraqi air attack failed due to rigid and inflexible mission planning, lack of sufficient target intelligence and the use of unsuitable General Purpose (GP) bombs. One F-4E was destroyed when it was almost cut in half in a strafing run on the ramp at Mehrabad airport, and another F-4 base, Hamedan, also suffered some damage.

The first Iranian air attack into Iraq saw the successful bombing of Al-Shoibiya (english translation: Ash-Shu'aiba) naval base, near the port of Um-Al Qassr, by four F-4s from Bushehr AB, using 1,000lb (450kg) bombs. Among the targets were several anti-shipping missile batteries. This Iranian retaliation was so swift that Iraqi air defence positions had been caught by surprise right across the flight route. The next day, up to 140 Iranian fighter-bombers, including significant numbers of F-4s from Bushehr, Tehran and Hamedan, attacked a number of Iraqi air bases and military installations with almost total impunity.

These first days of the war saw other air strikes against such targets as the military installations at the port city of Um-Al-Qassr. On one such mission a two-ship formation of F-4Es, each armed with six 750lb (340kg) GP bombs, attacked Iraqi port installations and anchored missile boats. Some 20 minutes later, an RF-4E took reconnaissance photos of the aftermath, which showed that heavy damage had been inflicted on ships and harbour installations.

The general tactic during such missions was to approach the target from different directions and then execute a pop-up and dive attack. On the return flight, one of the Phantoms was hit by a

SAM missile on the right wing, damaging some of its systems and control surfaces; despite this, the aircraft was still flyable. However, the fuel indicators did not work and the right wing caught fire. The runways of the nearest base were still damaged from the first day's bombing, so the crippled Phantom had to land on the unaffected part at a higher than normal speed. The tyres burst and the aircraft ran off the end

Above: *Although hampered by international sanctions, the Iranian F-4 fleet continued to press on into Iraq and in many cases returned home having sustained heavy damage. Take-offs were normally timed before dawn so the aircraft could reach their target area just after sunrise.*

Below: *An F-4E equipped with four AGM-65A Maverick TV-guided missiles. Most of the Iraqi Styx-equipped Osa missile boats were hit by Maverick missiles fired from IRIAF F-4Es, despite some difficulties encountered during the locking-on process.*

Mavericks in two waves, although Peykan too was finally sunk by a Styx missile.

Iran had purchased about 2,850 AGM-65As prior to the Islamic Revolution. As well as being used against sea targets, they were also carried to destroy bridges.

During the early phase of the war there were few IRIAF pilots – for example only two at Bushehr AB, who were trained and rated for firing Mavericks. Many pilots had to practise locking-on and firing the missiles during real combat missions.

Attack on Habbanieh Airfield

A month after the Iraqi invasion, two F-4D Phantoms were sent to attack the important air base of Habbanieh (Habbaniyah), 70 miles (112km) west of Baghdad. The flight was equipped with ECM pods and supported by F-14 Tomcats at the border, with an RF-4E on stand-by. Aerial refuelling was carried out at 13,000ft (3,960m) and the Phantoms then crossed the border to their target. One aircraft was shot down by a SAM over Baghdad and its crew taken prisoner. The second Phantom was able to evade an SA-6 missile by making an 11g turn, the missile passing across the aircraft's tail and wing. The crew realised that it was impossible to continue the attack and resorted to a pre-determined secondary target, the Al-Bakr oil refinery.

On the return leg, two Iraqi MiG-23s intercepted the F-4 and fired air-to-air missiles; the Phantom, flying at very low altitude, jettisoned its drop tanks and made evasive manoeuvres. The MiGs finally broke off the pursuit, by this time the Phantom was very low on fuel and the crew declared an emergency, preparing to eject. Having no other alternative, the supporting stand-by Boeing 707 tanker crossed the border into Iraq to provide much-needed fuel for the starving F-4, which had only 700lb left.

During the early months of the war, the number of Iranian aircraft being shot down by Iraqi air defences was relatively low, mainly because the operators were so inexperienced. However, this rate increased as the conflict

Above: *F-4 gun camera footage of an attack on an Iraqi rear supply centre on May 15, 1984. Note the very low-flying Phantom's shadow and the explosions caused by the strike.*

Below: *An Iraqi SA-3 SAM battery in the vicinity of the Baghdad's Al Rashid air base is unaware of the low-flying Iranian RF-4E. Note that the missile launchers are pointing away from the incoming recce aircraft, the shadow of which is visible at the bottom right – a sure sign that they have been caught by surprise. The fire control radar is to the centre and the early warning radar to the upper right. Date is unknown.*

progressed and newer systems were introduced. The flat topography of Southern Iraq meant that intruding Iranian aircraft were detected soon after entering the country. Deployment of newly-purchased low-altitude Crotale and Roland SAMs in and around Nasseriyeh (Nassariyah) AB and other militarily significant sites, including the strategic city of Baghubeh (Ba'qubah) near Baghdad, during 1986-87, increased the capabilities of the Iraqi defences. The most impenetrable air defence network in Iraq was undeniably to be found protecting Baghdad. The city was surrounded by overlapping belts of SA-2/-3/-6/-8, Roland and Crotale SAMs, radar-guided AAA and MiG-21/-23 and -25 air defence fighter interceptors.

On March 19, 1982, a high-altitude eight-aircraft strike formation of Phantoms was bounced and engaged by an Iraqi MiG-25 Foxbat from a distance of 60 miles (97km), and was also simultaneously illuminated by air defence radars. A number of SA-2 'telegraph poles' were seen passing through the formation, but all exploded at higher altitude, having been decoyed by the Phantom ECM pods. However, one was hit by an AAM fired from the Foxbat, shattering the canopy, causing the right engine to shut down, and badly damaging the fuselage. Nevertheless, the pilot managed to land safely.

The Iraqis also practised a tactic of setting up ambushes inside Iran at the border areas and pulling Iranian aircraft into the Iraqi airspace. Then Iraqi Mirage F1 or MiG-25 fighters equipped with long-range missiles would intercept them. Some Iranian F-4s were shot down using this tactic, particularly over the northern Persian Gulf. Iranian Phantoms and F-14A Tomcats also used to take advantage of such co-operative tactics; F-4s acting as the prey and F-14s as the hunters. This is contrary to previous reports in Western publications, where it had been suggested that Tomcats acted as prey for hunter Phantoms.

Striking H-3

Six months into the war, and after numerous successful attacks against their airfields, the Iraqis pulled back their most important assets into the Western airfields to prevent Iranian fighter-bombers from reaching them. Aware of this, perhaps from Israeli-supplied intelligence, IRIAF planned an air attack on the important strategic airfield of H-3 (Al-Valid or Al-Walid) and its satellite bases near the Iraqi-Jordanian border. Ten F-4Es flown by pooled elite Phantom crews from various bases – supported by F-14s, F-5s, the airborne command post and several Boeing KC 707 and KC 747 tankers – were tasked with this very difficult mission. On April 4, 1981, eight strike aircraft departed Tabriz AB, accompanied by two airborne reserves, which returned later. The Phantoms flew through the mountains of Northern Iraq and met up with one or two IRIAF KC 707-3J9C tanker(s) at very low altitude over the furthest reaches of north-west Iraq for refuelling.

It was not revealed until a few years ago, that the tanker aircraft had actually been waiting at Istanbul International Airport for the appropriate rendezvous time, then clandestinely diverted from international commercial corridor while apparently returning to Iran. It then went on to cross the Iraqi border and reach the rendezvous point with the Phantoms, staying at low altitude in western Iraq for their return. None of the hastily-scrambled Iraqi fighters were able to intercept the attacking Phantoms and all returned safely. It was later claimed that this air strike inflicted heavy losses on the Iraqi Air Force, including destroying or badly damaging 48 heavy bombers, fighters and helicopters, as well as destroying three large hangars, several HASs and two radar emplacements. As for another important mission late in the war, during Operation Valfajr-10, IRIAF F-4 Phantoms attacked and bombed Baghdad's Tamuz nuclear reactors for a second time.

Weapons

IRIAF used various weapons options in conjunction with its F-4 Phantom operations. They included general purpose bombs; such as 500lb Snakeye (x12) to 750lb (x6) and 1,000lb (x6) GP or retard versions. AIM-7E Sparrow and AIM-9P/J Sidewinder missiles were also carried regularly for air defence and fighter escort missions. Other weapons

This heavily damaged F-4E had crash landed but was later repaired and returned to flying status. The extended ejection rails indicate that the crew had ejected from the aircraft prior to it reaching a stop.

Above: *The IRIAF regularly undertook aerial refuelling at night and at low altitude, and/or in adverse weather conditions, using minimum radio communication, and sometimes in total radio silence. In many cases, receiver aircraft were forced to keep their radars turned off to comply with electromagnetic silence. Here an F-4E tanks up from one of the IRIAF's 12 KC 707-3J9Cs.* Below: *An Iranian F-14A Tomcat armed with an air-to-air version of the Hawk missile is keeping formation with an F-4E Phantom. During the war, these two aircraft co-operated closely in the interception role – one acting as prey and the other as hunter.*

included the AGM-65A Maverick used in conjunction with TISEO electro-optical sensor, BL 755 cluster bomb customised for low-altitude delivery, Napalm tanks and LAU-61 rocket launchers. IRIAF F-4Ds also used the SUU-23 gun pods to good effect.

Two IRIAF F-4D Phantoms were tasked with striking a logistically important bridge near Basreh (Basrah) on September 29, 1981, employing LGBs. They used a buddy-lasing tactic, one acting as target designator at about 13,000ft equipped with AVQ-9 Pave Light laser designator. The target was hit, but a short time later an SA-6 missile homed in on the designating aircraft. Both crew ejected as the aircraft was destroyed.

RF-4E - Unarmed Straggler

At the start of the war, the IRIAF had 15 RF-4E unarmed PhotoPhantoms based at the 1st Fighter Base in Mehrabad, Tehran. One had been lost before the war, having been shot down by a rebel Man-Portable Air Defence System (MANPADS) over the South Yemen in 1977. Reconnaissance aircraft, especially RF-4Es, were considered to be high-value assets, and were in short supply. Therefore, the Iraqi air defences went to a great deal of effort to shoot these recce aircraft down – losses were high and it is believed that only one or two RF-4Es remain airworthy.

One RF-4E, call sign Arash 11, took off at noon on January 27, 1983, from Mehrabad, accompanied by two F-14A Tomcats as top cover and a KC 707 tanker. These missions were mostly performed at low or medium altitude. The recce Phantom would use its RWR and ECM systems to determine the safest entry route, orbiting at 50,000ft until conditions were right and then descending to 2,000ft and accelerating to Mach 1.6 for the actual photo run. On this particular day, the RWR was lit up from all directions as the F-4 went towards its target, the main threat showing as an Iraqi Mirage F1 in the 11 o'clock position.

The Phantom ECM equipment was not programmed to counter Western-designed weapon systems and the aircraft was hit by two Matra Magic AAMs. Several other missiles were fired at the RF-4E, passing close by and exploding in mid-air. At this time, four 'bogeys' were closing on the Phantom from head-on and another from its 9 o'clock. Moments later, the back-seater noted a Matra Super 530 semi-active radar-guided AAM, painted in chequered white and orange – it is possible that the French had hastily delivered their development

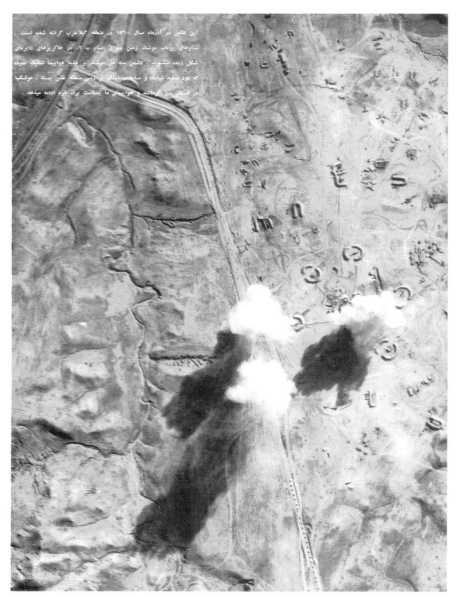

این عکس در آذرماه سال ۱۳۶۰ در منطقه گیلانغرب گرفته شده است.
سنگرهای پرتاب موشک ضدزمین بهوای دشمن سه ۲، در خاکریزهای دایرهای
شکل دیده میشود. دشمن سه تیر موشک بر علیه هواپیما شلیک نموده
که خود شده شلیک و سامانهسازی... زمین موشک تیر نشت پست، موشکها
... استایلین گردهان هواپیمای ما سلامت راه خود ادامه میدهد.

An Iraqi SA-2 battery fires three missiles towards Iranian recce aircraft in the Gilan-e-Gharb region, November-December 1981. The aircraft evaded the incoming missiles using its ECM equipment. IRIAF RF-4Es performed missions at mid-day to minimise shade in the pictures, the overhead sun helping to produce high-resolution images. These missions were mostly undertaken at low or medium altitudes.

arms embargo had restricted the supply of spare parts – consequently the Sparrow missile could not be fired most of the time. In addition, Iraqi aircraft ECM equipment was generally effective in breaking Iranian F-4 radar locks. According to Western sources, losses during the first nine months of the Iran-Iraq war were estimated to be 60 Phantoms, with many more being out of action due to cannibalisation or lack of spare parts. The effects of the arms embargo and the shortage of spare parts reduced the number of Phantoms available for combat. IRIAF and Iran Aircraft Industries (IACI) personnel did an incredible job of maintaining and overhauling every flyable aircraft – and rebuilding badly damaged fighters.

Iran was only able to keep its F-4s flying by scrounging spare parts and replacements from wherever it could. It was repeatedly reported that Israel secretly delivered Phantom spare parts to Iran, presumably thinking that by doing this it would help to keep Iraq occupied.

There were reports that Israel supplied critical spare parts for the Phantom's APQ-120 radar, which made it possible to fire the Sparrow semi-active radar-homing missile. In addition, Iran was able to purchase some arms supplies on the world market, either legally or illegally. In August 31, 1984, an Iranian F-4 pilot defected with his aircraft to Saudi Arabia, and upon investigation it was found to have components that came from Israel and several NATO countries. There were also several other F-4 defections to Iraq.

Escaping US Missiles

According to Iranian records, in early spring (March-April) 1988 (the US military claims it was August 8, 1987), an Iranian F-4 tried to approach a patrolling US Navy P-3C Orion. The Iranians later said that the F-4E Phantom from 9th Fighter Base, Bandar Abbas, armed with air-to-air missiles, was tasked with escorting a number of other Iranian Phantoms undertaking an unspecified strike mission within the Persian Gulf. That day, US forces in

rounds to Iraq to get them in use against Iranian aircraft. The missile hit the Phantom in the cockpit area, killing the pilot and forcing the injured back-seater to eject at 48,000ft (14,630m) while at supersonic speed. He evaded being captured and finally found his way to Iran the next day.

After 1982, Iraq improved its training procedures and was able to acquire newer and better arms from France, particularly the Dassault-Breguet Super Etendard and the Mirage F1C/EQ 5. The Mirage F1 was capable of firing the all-aspect Matra R.550 Magic/Magic2 AAM, with a reported 140° attack hemisphere, a head-on attack capability and high-g launch and manoeuvre capability, and a 0.14 to 6.2 mile (0.23 to 10km) range.

The APQ-120 radar in the Iranian F-4E Phantoms was partially inoperable because the

The Raytheon RIM-66A Standard missile has been modified in Iranian service for air-to-air and air-to-surface operations by the F-4. Iranian Phantoms are also modified to carry the Russian (AS-11 Kilter) Kh-58 anti-radiation missile with its associated targeting pod under the fuselage.

the area were also active and their warships warned off the low-flying Iranian strike package several times. The escort Phantom was scanning the area for any hostile activity, as the other F-4s attacked their targets one after the other and then left the area. Shortly after the last attacking aircraft returned, the escort fighter's RWR/RHAW indicated a missile lock. Moments later, a radar-guided missile, presumably a Sparrow, was launched towards the aircraft (it is said from a US aircraft). To break the radar lock, the Phantom jinked hard with maximum power, pulling a +12g turn – the missile exploded nearby, spraying the airframe with shrapnel, severing hydraulic lines and damaging the left engine.

The aircraft headed towards the nearest auxiliary airstrip, but on the way it again came under attack from behind. The Phantom tried hard to break the radar lock by flying low and taking evasive action; moments later, near the airstrip, another air-to-air missile passed the right side of the F-4, hitting the water and exploding. The aircraft managed to evade this and landed on the runway. Since the airstrip lacked a barrier facility, the pilot decided to get airborne again – despite the threat from the unknown fighter – and headed towards the main base. Despite partial hydraulic failure, engine problems and severe damage to the wing and fuselage, the Phantom remained controllable and finally landed in Bandar Abbas. This particular aircraft was rebuilt and returned to service after 6,000 man-hours and two and half months of work. According to the US military, an F-14A Tomcat from USS Constellation fired two Sparrow III missiles, one AIM-7F and one AIM-7M, from below 10,000ft (3,000m) towards the seemingly hostile Iranian aircraft without scoring a hit. The first missile's motor failed to ignite, and it fell harmlessly into the water. The second one appeared to track its target but by that time the two aircraft had closed to near the missile's minimum range and the Iranian F-4 successfully took evasive action.

Above: *Retaliatory strikes against Iraqi municipal installations, including propaganda value attacks on politically sensitive targets, were among the roles fulfilled by the IRIAF Phantoms – here an F-4E is seen over Northern Iran.*

Left: *This F-4D received a direct hit and was badly damaged during an unspecified combat mission. The fire spread to almost every part of the aircraft, but the crew remained with it and returned to base where they made an emergency landing. The Phantom was subsequently repaired and returned to service.*

Main F-4 operating bases

1st Fighter Base, Mehrabad, Tehran. Generating fighter and escort missions inside the border along western and south-western Iraq. It was also the main hub for tanker operations and aerial reconnaissance missions into Iraq and over battle fronts.

3rd Fighter Base, Hamedan (Shahrokhi, later Nojheh). Home to 31 and 32 Fighter Wings, this base was in charge of aerial support of the western front and suppression of the Kurdish uprising. Flying time from this base to Baghdad was 30 minutes. Due to its high sortie generation rate, Nojheh came under constant enemy bombing.

4th Fighter Base, Dezful (Vahdati) (mostly F-5). Because of its proximity to the Iraqi border, this base was constantly under artillery attacks and bombing.

6th Fighter Base, Bushehr. This base was mainly tasked with attacks on shipping in the northern and central parts of the Persian Gulf, escort and support of Iranian naval operations, and strike missions against Iraqi ports and naval vessels.

9th Fighter Base, Bandar Abbas. Mainly in charge of attacking shipping in the Persian Gulf, aircraft from this base monitored foreign military activities in and around the Strait of Hormuz, and provided escort and support of Iranian naval assets.

10th Fighter Base, Chabahar. Chabahar AB was in charge of monitoring the Sea of Oman and the Arabian Sea.

Surface vessel attack (naval interdiction and sea control) was a primary role for the IRIAF Phantoms during the Iran-Iraq war. Low-altitude operations over the Persian Gulf, sometimes near the Kuwaiti border, took place regularly. It was not uncommon to see the aircraft's exhaust gases produce wake on the water. Phantoms flew at between 200-400ft above the sea surface, doing around 400-550kts, they would then pop up and fire their missiles.

Weaseling its way

René J Francillon **looks at the F-4G and how it was used during the Cold War and Gulf War.**

DEVELOPED IN the mid-1970s as the Wild Weasel V to meet requirements stemming from combat experience during the Southeast Asia war, the Advanced Wild Weasel F-4G saw its capabilities honed to perfection during the 1980s to blunt a feared Warsaw Pact offensive in Central Europe and for a North Korean rush across the 38th Parallel. However, it gained its combat spurs in the early 1990s during DESERT STORM and the follow-on SOUTHERN WATCH and PROVIDE COMFORT when it wreaked havoc on Iraqi air defences.

Modified from an F-4E-43-MC airframe, 69-7254, the development aircraft for the Advanced Wild Weasel F-4G, was fitted with the AN/APR-38 warning and attack system by McDonnell Aircraft (MCAIR). It first flew on December 6, 1975, and deliveries of production standard F-4Gs modified from F-4Es by the Ogden Air Logistics Center at Hill AFB, Utah, began in April 1978 with the first F-4Gs going to the 39th Tactical Fighter Training Squadron, 35th Tactical Fighter Wing, at George AFB, California. (For additional

The F-4G Wild Weasel Phantom could carry an impressive array of ordinance, as is illustrated here. Below the port wing are an AGM-88 HARM and an AGM-65 Maverick, while below the starboard wing are an AGM-45 Shrike and an AIM-7 Sparrow air-to-air missile. An ALQ-119 self-protection electronic countermeasures pod is carried on the forward fuselage station. MCDONNELL

Left: *Two Wild Weasel Phantoms, from different units, the 52nd TFW at Spangdahlem and the 35th TFW at George AFB, pictured over a burning oil well in Kuwait shortly after* DESERT STORM *had ended in 1991.* VIA GERT KROMHOUT

Below: *The very first F-4G was modified from F-4E-43-MC serial number 69-7254 and this aircraft is seen here outside the McDonnell Douglas facility at St Louis, Missouri. The aircraft first flew on December 6, 1975, but was eventually retired by the USAF's 561st FS in 1992, entering the boneyard at AMARC on June 5. The aircraft has since become part of the drone programme and departed to Marconi Flight Systems for QF-4 conversion in mid-1999.* KEN DELVE COLLECTION

details, refer to *Wild Weasel Phantoms* published in the July 1994 issue of our sister publication, *AIR International*.)

To provide the Advanced Wild Weasel with its electronic brain, MCAIR integrated a Texas Instruments computer, an IBM radar warning system, and other components into the purpose-developed AN/APR-38 radar homing and warning set (RHAWS). First fitted experimentally to two EF-4Ds – 66-7647 and 66-7635 – the AN/APR-38 was optimised to locate and identify radars associated with surface-to-air missile sites and AAA batteries and to prioritise threats automatically. It was later brought up to AN/APR-47 standard under the Performance Update Program (PUP) initiated in the mid-1980s. By replacing the original on-board computer with a Unisys CP-1674 digital processor, display capability jumped to 20 times that with the APR-38, memory was increased eight-fold, and signals were processed five times faster.

Central Europe Tactics

During the 1980s, tactics evolved as it was determined that reliance on anti-radiation missiles (AGM-45 Shrike, AGM-78 Standard ARM, and, primarily, AGM-88 HARM) launched against guidance radars would be insufficient to eliminate the threat in its entirety. Even if the anti-radiation missiles succeeded in destroying the guidance radars, SAMs could still be launched ballistically or with guidance from remote sites. Hence, hunter-killer teams trained together, with F-4Gs going after the guidance radars, while F-4Es completed the task by destroying the now-blinded missiles with AGM-65 Maverick missiles, CBUs or conventional bombs. With the 52nd TFW in Germany, the effectiveness of these hunter-killer teams was increased when the F-4Es were replaced by F-16Cs, beginning in October 1987.

As described in the *USAF Fighter Weapons Review* by Capt Dan Hampton, an F-16C pilot with the 23rd TFS, while training to blunt a feared Warsaw Pact onslaught, the 52nd TFW would rely primarily on four-ship and six-ship formations with equal numbers of F-4Gs and F-16Cs. With fixed SAM sites deep behind enemy lines being taken care of by other means, hunter-killer teams were to patrol their assigned Restricted Operation Zone (ROZ) along the forward line of own troops (FLOT)/forward edge of battle area (FEBA).

While in the ROZ, the F-4Gs were to use their AN/APR-38s (later -47s) to pinpoint mobile SAM sites and their AGM-88Bs to destroy the radar associated with these sites.

The multi-tasked F-16Cs were to:
(1) Provide close escort for the F-4Gs using gun and Sidewinders,
(2) Destroy missile and AAA batteries with Maverick missiles and gravity ordnance, and
(3) Supplement the F-4Gs as HARM-shooters.

In that last capacity, F-16Cs were far less capable than their F-4G team-mates, as they were not fitted with RHAWS and were single-seaters. However, they could fire AGM-88s in two modes. In the 'range known' mode, AGM-88s were to be used against radar at fixed sites or previously located mobile sites, in which case, targeting information would be programmed into the HARM system by the F-16C prior to the mission. In the 'range unknown' mode, F-16Cs depended on the

F-4Gs to detect the enemy guidance radar, determine its location and range, and pass that information to the Fighting Falcon pilot. That often proved cumbersome and time-consuming, forcing the 'electric jets' to fly closer to SAM sites. By contrast, Advanced Wild Weasel F-4Gs have far more flexibility, as specific threat and band information can be transferred instantly to the AGM-88 from the AN/APR-47.

DESERT STORM *Tactics*

During DESERT SHIELD, Coalition planners had identified the destruction of KARI, the French-built command and control system named after Irak (the French word for Iraq – spelled backward) as the top priority. The next priority was the suppression of Iraq's radar-guided SAMs to enable Coalition aircraft to operate with relative impunity from medium altitudes, out of range of most AAA and MANPADS. Accordingly, during the first night of Operation DESERT STORM, the F-4Gs of the 35th TFW (Prov) were sent out in force. Going after guidance radar, 'painting' the night sky all the way to Baghdad after Iraqi defenders mistook decoys and drones for Coalition aircraft, Advanced Wild Weasel F-4Gs launched no fewer than 118 HARMs during the first night. The 'rain' of AGM-88s continued nearly unabated, night and day, during the first week, with almost half of the HARMs expended during the entire war being launched between January 17 and 23, 1991. Iraqi radar activity declined precipitously. To all intents and purposes, the threat of Iraqi radar-guided missiles, just like that of Iraqi fighters, had disappeared by the end of the first week. The Coalition owned the sky.

To accomplish this outstanding result, the USAF's lethal SEAD (suppression of enemy air defences) role was initially undertaken by F-4Gs operating alone or, alongside F-4Es and

'Few will deny that during the Gulf War the F-4Gs were among the most effective Coalition aircraft.'

Above: *Effective countermeasures are crucial to staying alive in the deadly SEAD role. The AN/ALQ-131 jamming pod was a common sight beneath the F-4G and is still in widespread use today.* AFM COLLECTION

Below: *An unarmed 52nd FW F-4G taxies past the sunsheds at Dhahran International Airport in September 1992. The 52nd FW was heavily tasked with patrolling both the northern and southern no-fly zones over Iraq, a role it still performs today but now solely with the F-16CJ.* KEN DELVE COLLECTION

F-16Cs, as part of hunter-killer teams. Unlike tactics developed earlier to blunt a Warsaw Pact offensive in Central Europe, and calling for operations from the friendly side of FEBA, Wild Weasels had to penetrate as far as 250 miles (400km) into Iraq to take out radar-guided SAMs concentrated around strategic targets. Except for F-117 operations, for which only minimal Wild Weasel support was provided (in sharp contrast to what was required during ALLIED FORCE in Serbia eight years later), mass raids required the inclusion of Wild Weasel hunter-killer teams.

As reported by Capt Hampton in the previously-mentioned report to the *USAF Fighter Weapons Review*, the composition of the hunter-killer teams changed after the eighth day, when the Iraqis drastically reduced their reliance on radar-guided SAMs, and planners switched emphasis from SEAD to DEAD (Destruction of Enemy Air Defences). Thereafter, the 35th TFW (Prov) in Bahrain and the 7440th Comp Wing (Prov) in Turkey typically flew 12-aircraft hunter-killer teams in support of day strike packages and eight-aircraft teams in support of night operations. When operating with 12 aircraft (six F-4Gs and six F-16Cs), the first two pairs were dedicated HARM and/or Shrike shooters operating in the traditional SEAD role. The next two pairs carried HARMs and Mavericks to remove predetermined targets, while retaining the ability to respond to enemy radar activities. The remaining four aircraft were F-16Cs loaded with CBUs and dumb bombs for dedicated DEAD strikes to obliterate missile and AAA batteries. In the process, CBU-57s proved devastatingly effective.

Complementing lethal strikes against Iraqi air defence were deception activities. To trick Iraqi monitoring of Coalition radio traffic into believing that AGM-88s had been launched,

The end of a distinguished career came on March 22, 1996, when the final examples of the F-4G were retired from frontline service by the 561st FS/57th FW at Nellis AFB, Nevada. F-4G 69-7295 was suitably inscribed to mark the occasion before being retired to AMARC on March 26. It was subsequently converted to a QF-4G drone at Mojave and assigned to the 475th WEG at Tyndall AFB, Florida.

Wild Weasel crews occasionally called 'Magnum' even when not firing HARMs. So feared were these missiles, that the Iraqi missileers promptly shut down their missile guidance radars upon hearing the dreaded 'Magnum' call. In the end, the results were the same; Iraqi radar-guided defences were no longer a factor – they had either been destroyed or removed to safety for later use.

Much Lamented Weasels

Few will deny that during the Gulf War the F-4Gs were among the most effective Coalition aircraft. Based at Sheikh Isa AB in Bahrain and Incirlik AB in Turkey, they flew 2,678 sorties, during which they launched most of the 1,067 AGM-88s expended by the USAF (in addition, Navy and Marine aircraft respectively launched 661 and 233 AGM-88s). Only one F-4G was lost in combat operations, 69-7571 crashing on January 19, 1991, due to fuel starvation after one of its tanks had been punctured by hostile fire and weather prevented

the aircraft from being air refuelled. The crew ejected safely over Saudi Arabia. Quite significantly, only one of the five Coalition aircraft lost to Iraqi radar-guided SAMs went down in spite of F-4G support. The other four had been flying without the benefit of Wild Weasel protection.

Nevertheless, 43 days after DESERT STORM ended, the Department of Defense announced that F-4Gs would be withdrawn from active duty units by January 1, 1993. A reduced number of F-4Gs were to be assigned to two ANG squadrons, one in Idaho and one in Nevada, while other F-4Gs were to be converted as QF-4G drones by Tracor Flight Systems (now Marconi Flight Systems) at Mojave Airport in California. However, the need for continuing operations over no-fly zones in Iraq (SOUTHERN WATCH and PROVIDE COMFORT) led to a partial reversal of this decision in order to maintain F-4G detachments with the 4404th Composite Wing (Provisional) at Dhahran RSAFB and the 7440th Comp Wg (Prov) at Incirlik AB.

To meet this need, although the Idaho ANG's 190th FS was declared Mission Ready with F-4Gs on October 1, 1992, plans to convert the Nevada ANG squadron from RF-4Cs to F-4Gs were cancelled. Meanwhile a new active duty squadron, the 561st FS, was activated with F-4Gs at Nellis AFB on February 1, 1993, and the departure of the F-4Gs with the 52nd FW was delayed until February 18, 1994. Proving their mettle, the 'Guardsmen' made two combat deployments to Saudi Arabia and two to Turkey between March 1993 and December 1995. They fired their first AGM-88B against an Iraqi radar on June 29, 1993, during a sortie from Dhahran. In addition, the ID ANG ran the F-4G Training Unit to train Wild Weasel crews for its own needs and those of the active duty 561st FS.

However, the F-4Gs were getting increasingly costly to man and maintain. Although no replacement with equal capabilities had been provided (F-16CJs fitted with the AN/ASQ-213 HARM Targeting System [HTS] are said to provide less than 80% of the F-4G capability), the last of the Weasels had to go. The 561st Fighter Squadron disposed of its F-4Gs and was deactivated on April 2, 1996. In Idaho, the 190th Fighter Squadron converted to A-10As and flew its last F-4Gs to AMARC on December 12, 1995. Both squadrons and their still unmatched F-4Gs were greatly missed during ALLIED FORCE.

The last six 52nd FW F-4Gs returned from Dhahran, after Operation SOUTHERN WATCH duties on March 30, 1993. Here, the 81st FS CO, Lt Col Dan Shealer is greeted as he climbs down from his jet after the long journey home. GERT KROMHOUT